There's a Bulldozer
on Home Plate

There's a Bulldozer on Home Plate

A 50-Year Journey in Minor League Baseball

MILES WOLFF

McFarland & Company, Inc., Publishers
Jefferson, North Carolina

ISBN (print) 978-1-4766-9017-9
ISBN (ebook) 978-1-4766-4785-2

LIBRARY OF CONGRESS AND BRITISH LIBRARY
CATALOGUING DATA ARE AVAILABLE

Library of Congress Control Number 2022061521

© 2023 Miles Wolff. All rights reserved

No part of this book may be reproduced or transmitted in any form or by any means, electronic or mechanical, including photocopying or recording, or by any information storage and retrieval system, without permission in writing from the publisher.

Front cover: Miles Wolff, owner of the Québec Capitales baseball team, in 2004 (Quebec City *Le Soleil*)

Printed in the United States of America

*McFarland & Company, Inc., Publishers
Box 611, Jefferson, North Carolina 28640
www.mcfarlandpub.com*

To Michelle, Hoffman, and Claire

August 20, 2009: conversation between league president and commissioner

"We've got problems in Nashua. We probably won't have a game there tonight."

"What are you talking about?"

"A bulldozer is parked on home plate."

"A bulldozer? Why doesn't somebody move it?"

"It's the city's, and the mayor has the keys. She says she won't move it until the owner pays his rent for last month."

"Can't she wait until the end of the season? I talked to her earlier. The owner doesn't have the money now, but I promised her we'd get the lease paid sometime this fall."

"She doesn't want to wait. She's making a statement and has the media out taking pictures of her bulldozer. I think it's an election year."

"Damn. We've only got a week before the season is over. Let's see if we can't move the home games to the visiting team's park so we can work on a solution. Is it a big bulldozer?"

"Really big."

Table of Contents

Prologue — 1

1. "You Have a Bed in the Navy" — 3
2. Pack the Park — 10
3. Victoria, Toronto, Anderson and Others — 23
4. Jacksonville, Richmond, Vancouver and Victoria — 32
5. Durham — 49
6. The Movie — 66
7. "You Want to Buy the Bulls?" — 70
8. "What's That Round Piece of Rubber For?" — 76
9. Where in the Hell Is Thunder Bay? — 86
10. Who Would Want to Play Independent Ball? — 102
11. "Let's Start Our Own League" — 110
12. Growth — 115
13. *Baseball America* — 124
14. Quebec — 130
15. What's a Road Team? — 140
16. Ottawa — 147

Epilogue — 163
Appendix: Careers in Independent Baseball (1993–2019) — 167
Index — 173

Prologue

It was a bit Wild West, it was the circus that came to town, and it was selling something that didn't exist. But it wasn't a con, it was a dream. It was the belief that I could come to a town and make my dream become its dream. It was giving a city something it didn't need, having it fall in love with the dream and ultimately making it come true. The key was to make others believe. The role was that of a Johnny Appleseed, coming to a town, searching for fertile ground. In this case the ground needed to be a person, a mayor, a leading citizen, or a journalist who would till the soil. And then the seeds would be sown. The picture would be painted, and then the ground would be watered with the history of a glorious past, and if the elements were right, the dream would start to grow.

In the movie and Broadway show *The Music Man*, Professor Harold Hill travels the Midwest, convincing small cities that they needed a boys' marching band complete with instruments and uniforms. The show's producer and writer was Iowan Meredith Willson, and the story is set in River City, Iowa. It was in a river city in Iowa, where the dream would start to flourish.

The city was Sioux City, Iowa, on the banks of the Missouri River. It had once been a leading city in the Upper Midwest, but meat packing and other industries had departed, and the city had grown little in recent decades. A meeting is set with the Sioux City economic development director. Unfortunately, the director does not know the area well, a situation that is a bit incongruous, and as he searches for an old ballpark site, he drives up the wrong access road to the interstate. As he heads directly into oncoming traffic, frightened whimpers alert him that he has made a mistake. A U-turn on the median solves the problem and the car heads back to town. There is nothing to find. The baseball facility had been torn down years before, and clearly it is time to write off Sioux City as a potential site. Sioux Falls, South Dakota, is 85 miles north, and perhaps that city has potential.

But seeds have been thrown in Sioux City and they are starting to

Prologue

germinate. Earlier in my visit, I had met with the mayor of Sioux City who instructed the novice economic development director to show potential ballpark sites. That night in Sioux Falls, the mayor calls and wants to meet once more. He has heard about the less-than-successful mission with the economic development director. The flight from Sioux Falls is scheduled for mid-morning, but the Sioux City mayor insists that he and the mayor pro tem need to meet with me, and they drive up at 5 a.m. to meet before the flight departs. The mayor wants a team for his city. At this point there is no league and there are no other committed cities, but he is ready to bring Sioux City into a phantom league.

I am selling a promise of a baseball league that failed two decades earlier and a type of baseball that had gone out of business forty years before. It is independent baseball, professional baseball without any major league help. For nearly half a century, minor league baseball had been the ward of major league baseball, surviving only with the millions of dollars that the big-league clubs dole out annually. The big leagues are not generous because they believe that baseball should be a national sport, the "National Pastime," as sportswriters love to call the game. In truth, MLB owners have never been accused of being visionary, doing what is best for the sport. They pump money into the minor leagues because they need a training ground for players. Football and basketball have college athletics as their farm systems. Baseball needs the minors. The pitch for a new league is simple. Baseball in mid-sized cities can survive without the big leagues. The economics can work. When baseball teams play to win, not develop players, it can be an attractive sport and draw crowds. In the right cities, with the right ownership, and the right direction, independent baseball will survive.

In the morning meeting with the mayor of Sioux City, my enthusiasm about the potential for professional baseball in his city is limited. The visit had been a bust. He has no ballpark, and the city is not flush with funds. It will take considerable public funding to build a new stadium from scratch. The search in the Upper Midwest was for older stadiums that could be refurbished. It is difficult to believe that a city will build a new facility for a league that doesn't exist. Where is the money? When the question is posed, he answers that he will switch funding for projects that are in the current city budget. As he confidently puts it, "Millions for baseball, not a dime for the arts." However, he needs to be certain that there will be five other cities and a real league. If that can happen, he will spend $3 million on a new stadium. I quickly fall in love with Sioux City. A new league will be a reality if I can find five other cities willing to come along.

1

"You Have a Bed in the Navy"

The dream of an independent league had been on the fringes of my mind for the twenty or so years of my involvement in minor league baseball. I had been a general manager, a play-by-play announcer, and a team owner. I knew the business of the minors. Baseball's Winter Meetings in 1990 convinced me that something needed to be done. The big leagues were threatening to do away with the minor league system unless some fairly onerous demands were met. Being on the minor league executive committee as the Single-A representative, I was part of the negotiating committee. In contentious meetings with MLB officials their lawyers were unpleasant, unyielding, and uninformed. I believed that the minors could call the big leagues' bluff. They wouldn't do away with minor league baseball. Controlling the Single-A votes, we could defeat the MLB proposal.

At a cocktail party the evening before the vote, a friend from the major league negotiating committee pulled me aside and let me know that the commissioner's office was deadly serious. It was making arrangements with college baseball programs to use their facilities during the summer, and enough spring training facilities under big-league control were available to develop a scaled-down minor league system of their own. He realized this proposal would financially cost the big leagues more than the minor league system currently in effect. But he stressed that MLB's ego would not allow a loss to minor league baseball. MLB had recently lost labor negotiations to the umpires and to the players' union.

The vote of the Class A leagues to approve MLB's proposal was the swing vote. The next morning, with much distaste, I voted "yes" to the majors' demands. The minors were saved, but what would be the long-term consequences? After these negotiations, it was clear that doing business with the majors was never going to be a positive experience. An option was needed for leagues and cities that might ultimately lose their teams with the new demands of MLB. That option could be independent

There's a Bulldozer on Home Plate

baseball leagues, circuits that had no ties to the big leagues. It would be different and expensive, but someone needed to show that the minor leagues need not always bow down to big-league demands.

The problems associated with forming an independent league appeared immense. Where were the cities? Where was competent ownership? Would there be quality players willing to come to a league without major league ties? How could hundreds of thousands of dollars be added to a minor league budget and have teams survive? Yet, two years later an independent league was in business. No one knew what to expect. But those who had bought into the dream knew it would be different, exciting, and a chance to do something special in a game they loved. It was all that and more. Even the names were special: the Winnipeg Goldeyes, the Sioux Falls Canaries, the Thunder Bay Whiskey Jacks.

And the players... Who would have thought that Darryl Strawberry, Jack Morris, Oil Can Boyd, Pedro Guerrero, Bull Durham, and a hundred other big leaguers would trek to the Upper Midwest to play in a league that wasn't part of organized baseball? The baseball was great, and every season something new and different appeared. St. Paul had a pig that took balls to the umpires. Ila Borders became the first female pitcher to win a game in professional baseball. A nun gave massages during the games, and Minnie Minoso became one of the few professional players in baseball history to appear in five decades of baseball when he came to bat as a pinch hitter. Books were written about the league, magazines had special features, and *60 Minutes* and other national TV shows and correspondents traveled out to the heartland to discover this upstart league. It was wild. It was wonderful. It was the Northern League.

Greensboro, 1954

You are ten years old, and your family has moved to a new neighborhood. You have not met any kids in the neighborhood, and you are a bit lost. Then, something happens. Your parents make a trip to Baltimore, where you were born, and when they come back, they bring you a hat from the Baltimore Orioles. You have never really liked baseball, but you have this hat. It is the first year of the Baltimore Orioles in the major leagues, and something clicks. You start reading the morning paper to find out about the team. They lose, but you become a fan. Then in your Sunday school class, the teacher gives all the kids in the class a pack of ten tickets to the Greensboro Patriot games. The Patriots are a Class B team in the Carolina League. You were meant to learn about religion in this class, but you have emerged with something more important ... baseball tickets. Your teacher is one of the stockholders in the

1. "You Have a Bed in the Navy"

local club and the treasured gift he has given you is really an effort to get more fans in the stands. It doesn't matter. Baseball has put its hook in you. You have two teams and your life will become consumed.

Baseball is usually given from father to son, but your dad is only a casual fan. Your mother is less so and your two older sisters have no interest at all. The baseball you have found is yours alone. You go to the game by yourself and sit on the third base side. You listen to the other fans and learn how to yell at the umpires and opposing players. You scramble for foul balls in the splintered bleacher seats. It is a simpler time and your parents let you walk the mile and a half to and from the game by yourself. You are now, in your mind, an adult, an equal of everyone else in the stadium, and baseball transports you to a new existence. It is special. Baseball will be your life.

At the age of 12, I was cut from Little League tryouts for the third straight year. It was becoming clear that perhaps becoming a major league player was not on the horizon. For most young boys, this rejection would be the signal to go to other sports or other interests. But baseball had hooked me, and I followed the Baltimore Orioles religiously. The Greensboro Patriots (and later Greensboro Yankees) were also my team, and their games drew me to old World War I Memorial Stadium. Somehow, the dream of working in minor league baseball started in this period. At age 15 I went to the G-Yanks' front office to ask for a part-time job. But I fumbled and mumbled the inquiry, and instead bought a book of tickets.

Watching the promotions, I tried to figure out why fans did or did not come to the games. With crowds of less than 500 most nights, it seemed strange that more people did not show up. Was I that different? Some of the promotions did draw crowds. Max Patkin, the baseball clown, was always a good draw, and Jackie Price, the remarkable hitting showman, made a yearly visit to the ballpark and respectable crowds attended. And there were the free nights, when attendance was great, but the free folks never seemed to return.

Occasionally, something might move the needle. Pony Night was one promotion that worked with a mangy-looking mini-steed given to an unlucky child. Guilford Dairy Night, with its free tickets, was a regular occurrence that could cause a spike in attendance. One Sunday afternoon, the team scheduled a Tropical Pet Day, as goldfish and gerbils were given away. The grand prize was a boa constrictor, and I held tightly to a ticket stub hoping to win. Midway through the game, it dawned on me that if I did win, I would have to take the snake home. My mother would not be pleased. Hopes changed and I desperately prayed

There's a Bulldozer on Home Plate

that someone else would win. Luck was on my side, and I did not have to face my mother and explain a boa constrictor.

Fascination with minor league baseball continued until it was time to enter college. My parents did not know of my desire to work in minor league baseball, and approval of that career path would probably have been less than enthusiastic. Also, at that time, no sports administration programs existed that might guide a person in that direction. Johns Hopkins University in Baltimore became the choice. I had heard that the center on the school's basketball team was 6'2". I was a 6'2" center in high school with little playing time. Perhaps a mediocre basketball career could continue. The school also offered financial aid. Most importantly, the Baltimore Orioles' offices were only a few miles from campus. This could be the avenue to enter baseball. Each spring for the next four years, I would walk to Memorial Stadium and meet with Harry Dalton or Lou Gorman, the farm directors of the Orioles. They were pleasant and gave good advice. My thoughts were strong on dropping out of college if a baseball job appeared, but nothing developed.

The four years at Hopkins were good. Most of my fellow students were pre-meds, spending all waking hours immersed in study, hoping to get into a top medical school. This left open all the other activities on campus, and it was easy to take advantage of these opportunities. I did become a 6'2" center on the basketball team and never started a game. My career high scoring was 6 consecutive points against M.I.T. The coach quickly took me out of the game. I was involved in the student radio station, WJHU, and became the play-by-play announcer of both lacrosse and football. The professors were great and after I graduated with a major in liberal arts, it was time to make some decisions.

The Vietnam War was expanding, but President Johnson promised that the "light is at the end of the tunnel" and the war would soon be over. With the military draft still looming, it appeared prudent to apply for another student deferment by going to graduate school. Surely the war would be over in another year. At the University of Virginia, my field of study was Southern U.S. history, but I felt like a phony. Virginia had an excellent history department, and serious graduate students were working toward their degrees. My purpose was not history but to avoid the draft. As I contemplated dropping out, the head of the department called me in. Somehow, he knew of the plan to leave school. He encouraged me to stay. The master's program was usually two years, but he suggested taking more courses, going to summer school, and graduating in a year. It made sense.

1. "You Have a Bed in the Navy"

The difficulty was writing my master's thesis. I did not want to spend the spring in the bowels of the library researching an obscure subject that no one really cared about. But the need was for something original. Looking for a topic, I saw that the Greensboro sit-ins had never really been studied or written about. The civil rights struggle was still active in 1966, and Greensboro had largely been forgotten. It had led to so much activism in the decade and deserved a closer look. Plus, it was in Greensboro and I could go home on weekends to do research.

Unfortunately, I had no contacts in the African American community in Greensboro. However, there was one white merchant in Greensboro whose clothing store catered mainly to Black students at North Carolina A&T University. One Saturday I wandered into his store to ask if he knew anyone I should talk to about the sit-ins. He was busy with a customer but when I was able to ask my question, he replied that I should talk to him. "I started the sit-ins," he stated, and he had me sit and brought out scrapbooks of newspaper clippings related to his involvement. He continued with his customer while I leafed through his scrapbooks. As a young man, he had worked to be the "World's Greatest Gate Crasher," and he had clippings of himself in the middle of the ring of championship boxing matches. He had photos of himself with Jackie Robinson and other civil rights legends and had worked against segregation in Greensboro for over a decade. In 1960 he had convinced four freshmen from A&T that trying to desegregate the lunch counter at the downtown Woolworth's was an action that could have positive results. The sit-ins in Greensboro led to massive protests across the South. I had found the motherlode of information on the sit-ins. My graduate thesis, "Lunch at the Five & Ten," would be published and go through four editions. It became the definitive work on the 1960 Woolworth sit-ins in Greensboro.

The draft was still a factor. Without a student deferment, it was inevitable I would have to serve. Despite President Johnson's assurances, the crazy Asian war was not over, and tens of thousands of young men were being sent to Vietnam. Many would never return. What were the options? A roommate from college had gone to Canada, but that did not appeal. My brother-in-law who had served in the Army did not recommend that branch of the service. "In the Army, you may have to sleep on the ground. You have a bed in the Navy." That was a logical reason. I was eligible to become an officer and signed up for the Navy. In early January 1967 I arrived at Officer Candidate School (OCS) in Newport, Rhode Island. It was cold, and marching in the snow made little sense. But it was the start of a great education.

There's a Bulldozer on Home Plate

In five months, I became an ensign and was assigned to Supply Corps school in Athens, Georgia. My preference would have been to be a line officer, but 20–20 eyesight was required. The Supply Corps was the business arm of the Navy. Fellow inductees at OCS who had graduated from the Wharton School of Business and other great MBA programs were desperate to become supply officers. They were ordered to ships. I was a history major with no training or education in business, but the Navy decided I was to be in the business side of running ships. One did not question the Navy brass who made these decisions. It was an unexpected education. I did not realize that food service, accounting, inventory, and much more were subjects that would transfer to the job of being a minor league GM.

The three years in the Navy were special. After six months of Supply Corps School, I served on two ships, the USS *Puget Sound* (AD-38), a destroyer tender under construction in Bremerton, Washington, and later on the USS *Charles P. Cecil* (DD-835), a World War II–era destroyer out of Newport. As a lowly ensign, I was given a department to run where my role was to give orders to chief petty officers and petty officers, some with 20 years' experience, who knew far more than I would ever know about accomplishing the job. How was I to prepare for this? These were amazingly accomplished individuals who didn't need a college degree to know how to run a ship worth hundreds of millions of dollars. No one ever asked where they received their degree. Being able to operate effectively was all that mattered. The good ones got things done, and all they needed was respect. That was easy to give.

After three years, I was discharged. It had been an extraordinary experience. I had joined the Navy and seen the world: Senegal, Mozambique, India, Seychelles, Bahrain, Brazil and more. I had learned a good deal about myself. The Navy thought it was training a supply officer, but the truth was that it trained a minor league GM. All the little details that I thought were unnecessary now made sense. Things that seemed as if it was only the Navy being picky really worked in real life. If feeding, paying, and supplying a ship for eight months in the Indian Ocean were possible, surely I could take care of a ballpark for a few summer months. It is three years of my life I would not trade for anything.

After discharge, it should have been time to get serious about a career, but it was not quite time. I drove across the country and visited Navy buddies. I spent the summer in Paris with my college roommate and his wife. He was a language student and we enrolled in a French school to study French. Paris was great, but the language for me would

1. "You Have a Bed in the Navy"

never be easy. By the fall, it was time to start trying to make an entry into baseball. I sent out letters but received few replies. I traveled to a Carolina League meeting, was introduced to all the owners, and made my pitch. Nothing seemed to come of this, but one owner, Marshall Fox, did remember me.

A month later, the farm director of the Atlanta Braves called Marshall Fox and asked for a recommendation on another job applicant. Fox told the farm director he had someone better and gave him my name. The day after Christmas, I flew to Atlanta and was interviewed by the farm director of the Braves. His name was Eddie Robinson, a former big-league first baseman. My mother was not a baseball fan, but when she and my father were first married, they would go to see the Baltimore Orioles when they were a minor league club. Eddie Robinson, the first baseman on the club, was her favorite player. A few days after the interview, I was hired.

The position was general manager of the Savannah Braves, the Double-A farm team owned by the Atlanta Braves. The pay was $600 a month. I was overjoyed and would have taken less. On January 2, 1971, I made the drive from North Carolina to Savannah, Georgia. Entering Savannah, the highway rises over a massive green bridge that crosses the Savannah River. On reaching the top of the bridge, the city spread out below. I had the feeling this was the magical city of Oz, and Savannah would be my city. I was finally in baseball.

2

Pack the Park

Branch Rickey, the great major league general manager and the father of baseball's farm system, once said, "Luck is the residue of design." You need to know what to do to put yourself in the right position, so that if luck comes your way you will be able to grab it. But sometimes, good fortune just happens.

I had come along at the right time. When I made my start in minor league baseball, the minors were at their lowest point since the middle of World War II. During the war years, many leagues folded because there simply weren't enough players to field teams. They had all been drafted. When peace arrived, baseball boomed, and in 1949, 438 cities had a minor league team. But in the 1950s, television and air conditioning became available to everyone, and by the 1970s, the minors had dwindled to 106 cities. It was a dying industry. Some officials at the major league level were advocating eliminating all but the Triple-A leagues. The big leagues could train the majority of the minor league players at spring training complexes in Florida and Arizona. Doing away with the lower minors made sense to big-league executives when they viewed the bad playing fields, inadequate lighting, and small, dirty, smelly clubhouses that populated minor league baseball.

In the early 1970s, universities were starting sports administration programs, but very few young people desired to work in minor league baseball. Minor league front offices were filled with older GMs who had started in the glory days of the minors in the late 1940s and early 1950s. Decades later, little energy or innovation existed among the old guard who were hanging on in minor league front offices.

The Atlanta Braves were one of the few major league organizations that owned their own minor league teams. Most big-league clubs worked with local ownership and did not have any financial interest in the day-to-day operations of the teams. The Braves had been hiring older, experienced GMs to run their teams but were dissatisfied. Some of these GMs pocketed a portion of the nightly receipts and many were

2. Pack the Park

unwilling to take direction from the big-league office. The Braves had begun hiring younger GMs and liked the results. They acquired the Savannah franchise in late 1970 and started the search for a new, young GM. I was one of the few candidates they found.*

The big-league Braves moved from Milwaukee to Atlanta in 1966, and this created a strong interest in the club in another Georgia town, Savannah. The Cleveland Indians had been the parent club in Savannah in 1970, averaging less than 500 fans in attendance per game. The Indians moved their club out of Savannah after that season. However, in the fall of 1970 a new mayor was elected in Savannah, John Rousakis, and he was bringing energy to the city. He made an appeal to the Braves, and they agreed to move their Double-A club from Shreveport to Savannah. The mayor pushed a major ticket drive, and he promised to put 10,000 fans in the ballpark on opening night.

The ballpark in Savannah, ancient Grayson Stadium, held 8,000 spectators. Filling a stadium that large would be difficult. The first month in Savannah, I began selling tickets and advertising in the community. Although folks were happy that the team was in town, there was no groundswell of ticket sales or sponsorships. In late February, I made an appointment to see the mayor. The outlook for 10,000 people in the stadium on opening night was bleak, and I needed his help.

Mayor Rousakis was not about to accept a pessimistic forecast on opening night attendance. In truth, he could not let it happen. He was on record as saying 10,000 people would be at the park for the opener. Rousakis was early in his political career, and he had staked too much in drawing the Braves to the city to show failure.

As mayors are wont to do, he formed a committee: the "Pack the Park Committee," and it began to show results. The group pushed opening night all over the city. With its help, we were able to arrange for the reigning Miss America, Phyllis George, to come and throw out the first pitch. Lou Brissie, a former World War II hero, major league veteran and Savannah pitching hero who had won 23 Sally League games for the team in 1947, agreed to come. The Braves sent the National League's 1970 batting champion, Rico Carty. Carty had broken his leg and was on Atlanta's disabled list. Everything clicked, and that night, April 15, a half dozen other minor celebrities attended. Every Little League team and Boy Scout troop were invited to come for free, and most showed

---

*In contrast to today, as the job seekers' seminar at each year's baseball Winter Meetings hosts at least 300 young people seeking any opportunity.

There's a Bulldozer on Home Plate

Savannah, Georgia. Grayson Stadium (formerly Municipal Stadium) has been the home of minor league baseball in Savannah since 1926. For many years, it also doubled as the football stadium for the city. The current grandstand was built as a WPA project in the 1930s.

up. By the second inning, fans, unable to find seats, were coming to the office to ask for their money back. It was a glorious evening.

When I began in baseball, I promised myself to only announce the correct attendance. I had seen too many teams announce inflated figures (known in the industry as "padding") for their crowds, and the official reported attendance was a joke. I was not going to pad. In the seventh inning of opening night, I had counted all the stubs and was overjoyed that 8,500 fans were in the ballpark when the mayor's chief of staff Al Henderson came into the office.

"Miles, what's the crowd tonight?" he asked.

"Al, we've got 8,522 here. This is just tremendous."

He shook his head. My impression was that he did not understand, and I repeated the figure. Al just smiled, looked me straight in the eye and quietly spoke. "Miles, there are 10,000 people here tonight."

I nodded slowly, swallowed hard and then picked up the phone. I called up to the press box. "Tonight's official attendance is 10,401."

The figure was repeated over the PA system. The crowd went wild,

2. Pack the Park

the mayor's office was pleased, and I was headed down the road of lies and deceit.

THE TEN COMMANDMENTS OF PADDING

1. *Thou shalt pad your stadium capacity.* Who really knows the exact capacity of your facility? If your park holds 5,000, publish that it holds 6,500. Then, if you have a nearly full stadium, you can announce that you have 6,351 when you actually have around 4,000. It is not only in baseball where this deception holds true. I have talked to a couple of Atlantic Coast Conference ticket managers who swear their basketball facilities never held what was announced.

2. *Thou shalt be consistent in your pad.* Don't fluctuate too much. If you're padding by 20%, do it every night. In half a season, you can ask your sportswriter for his estimate of the crowd, and he'll be able to give you your pad.

3. *Thou shalt not have turnstiles.* Who wants reality to intrude? Do count your ticket stubs at the end of the night because the money needs to balance.

4. *Thou shalt say you are using the American League system of attendance.* The National League counts only bodies in the park. The American League also counts no-shows and season tickets. If someone questions your count, you can say that the empty seats are season ticket holders who never showed up.

5. *Thou shalt not have individual seats throughout the park.* Certainly, you want good box and reserved seating, but in the bleachers, fans tend to spread out. 18 to 20 inches is the standard architects use to figure seating capacity. Rarely do spectators sit that closely in open bleacher seating. They put down coats and concession items. Also, the modern American rear end tends to be larger. A bleacher section can look totally packed with just a little over half capacity.

6. *Thou shalt publicize your pad.* If you're going to lie, you might as well make it a whopper. The folks who are modest about their attendance are probably telling the truth. But the big-time padders seem to win the awards. Two ex-minor league GMs who received national attention from their attendance ended up as major NBA executives.

7. *Thou shalt hope your team does not make the playoffs.* Well, not really, because it does help if your team wins. But most minor leagues have gate sharing in the playoffs, and that means the home team has to divulge the real attendance to the opposing team. At one Sally League playoff game, the crowd was announced at 4,000. This led to some heated exchanges when the visiting team was paid on a crowd of 1,500.

8. *Honor thy fellow GMs.* Don't try to fool them. They know if you're padding because they probably do it themselves. Keep things in line when they're around. One GM announced a crowd of 7,000 at an all-star game in a ballpark that sat only 3,200. The respect for him around the league was considerably lowered.

There's a Bulldozer on Home Plate

    9. *Be honest with yourself. Know the reality. Some GMs actually believe their pad, ticket sales statement notwithstanding.*
    10. *Thou shalt not lie. If you tell the truth, you will not have to remember commandments 1 through 9, and life will be simpler. You may not win awards, but everything will be easier.*

Opening Night was over, and the crowd was gone. I sat on the floor of my office, a small concrete bunker, counting money until late into the night. I loved it. This was going to be easy and I knew the crowds were going to continue to pour in. I was wrong. It was not going to be easy. The team had won the first night. Then, the team went a month without winning another game at home. It was a mediocre team with the best player being a 37-year-old shortstop. The attendance dropped swiftly.

Savannah is known for its afternoon thunderstorms. That year, without a full field tarp, we had 13 rainouts. The city did supply a part-time groundskeeper who often lamented that he didn't have a mule to drag the infield. He was not comfortable with his tractor. There was only one other full-time employee, a young secretary who was paid $70 a week. With the groundskeeper rarely around, the secretary and I covered the mound and home plate with heavy pieces of canvas before the afternoon showers. It did little good. The crowds dwindled to the same 500 a game the Savannah Indians had drawn the year before.

The traditional big promotion in Savannah was Union Paper Night. The Union Paper company, one of the largest employers in the city, bought out the stadium and distributed free tickets to employees and friends. On the first Union Paper night, a huge crowd attended. That night, our ticket taker who also counted the ticket stubs could not find an open space to count tickets and he went up to the press box where there was room to count.

The Union Paper Night tickets all had a lucky number printed on them, and ticket stubs were drawn to give out prizes. Some fans handed three or four tickets to the ticket taker in order that they might have a better chance of winning a prize. I knew that the count of ticket stubs would be exaggerated, and I told the ticket taker to come back to the office when he was finished so that I could adjust the count. I was ready to announce an attendance of around 8,000. Unfortunately, when the ticket taker finished counting and headed out of the press box to tell me the number, the sports editor asked him the count. He was told 14,201. The sports editor immediately grabbed the microphone of the PA system and announced that figure, telling the fans that this was the largest crowd in the history of Savannah baseball. Everyone cheered, excited

2. Pack the Park

that they were part of a record-setting event. There was no adjusting the figure.

That first season was a great learning year. Promotional ideas went well. From necessity, cutting the infield grass and dragging the infield became part of my education. The Braves brought me to Atlanta for a day to set up a concession menu and to give insight into what to sell. Ticketing, press releases and stadium cleanup became part of the experience. I was a one-man show, doing everything. Fortunately, the field manager was Eddie Haas. He had been a can't-miss prospect as a player until a serious injury derailed his career. Eddie had been managing in the minors for four years and knew the ropes. After every game, he would come to the office, drink a beer, and talk about the game and other aspects of baseball. He was a great teacher, thoughtful and steady, and would eventually manage in the big leagues.

Eddie let me know when some of my rookie ideas were not appropriate in a baseball setting. One Sunday I scheduled a "Pray for Pitching" promotion. The pitching staff that year was not world-class, and I concluded that only a higher power could help. If a fan brought a church bulletin to the game that day, he would be admitted for half price. The promotion worked as several hundred fans came to the game with a church bulletin. Eddie quietly let me know that this was not a great idea. His pitchers were unhappy. He explained that it "showed up" the pitching staff, and that it was best to encourage the players, not demean them. I understood.

That season was not particularly good on the field. The team ended up in next-to-last place, some 34 games out of first. Even with the 13 rainouts, attendance almost doubled from the previous season. I was a rookie and certainly made mistakes, but that fall, the *Sporting News* named me Double-A executive of the year. Perhaps the editors were swayed by the two large crowds, but it was a special honor, with the award being presented at baseball's Winter Meetings.

If the first year was great, the second year was even better. I now had a season under my belt with a better knowledge of what was needed. Sales grew, promotions were expanded, and attendance increased. Most importantly, the Atlanta Braves sent Clint "Scrap Iron" Courtney to Savannah as manager. Scraps was my childhood hero when he played with the Baltimore Orioles, and now I was going to be working with him. If Eddie Haas was steady and solid, Scraps was colorful and outrageous. The media loved him, and he made baseball fun. Clint Courtney was unique.

There's a Bulldozer on Home Plate

Scraps was always looking to shake up the establishment. In the middle of the season, he decided to put up a chicken-wire fence in deep right-center field to shorten the distance so that his hitters would have a better chance of hitting home runs. The media loved the idea, but league president Billy Hitchcock correctly ruled that this was illegal under baseball's official rules. I was ordered to take the rickety fence down. Scraps was fined $20, which outraged him, and he instructed me to pay the fine in pennies. After I lugged the pennies to the post office, the cost of postage was more than the fine. Scraps studied the rule book religiously, always hoping to catch the umpires in a mistake. Clint Courtney would have made a fine big-league manager.

Bulls Illustrated (April/May 1982)
Memories of Scrap Iron

The first time I ever saw Scrap Iron in person, he was wearing a Durham Bulls uniform. His playing days were just about over as he had been sent to Durham by the Houston Colt .45s as a player-coach. He was sitting in the dugout of aging Memorial Stadium in Greensboro where he was trying to bet Rusty Staub, Wally Wolf, or anyone on the Durham bench that he could throw a green walnut further than any of them could throw a baseball.

It was pre-game, and as I leaned over the chain link fence between the stands and the field, I listened to this squeaky, high-pitched, rural Louisiana voice boast that he could throw the walnut over the light towers deep behind the left-field fence. The players just laughed, but no one would bet him, leaving only two people convinced that he could do what he said, Scraps and me.

It has been close to seven years since Scraps died, and I'm always amazed at the strength of the memories. Clint Courtney was a major league catcher for ten years, and although he was Rookie of the Year in 1952, he spent most of his career with second-division clubs like the St. Louis Browns and the Washington Senators. His lifetime average was .268, and if the truth be known, he was at best only a journeyman catcher.

But Scraps was part of my early baseball consciousness, for he was the only catcher in the major leagues who wore glasses. Since I had just been prescribed my first pair of glasses, I assumed that Clint Courtney and I must be blood brothers, and I, too, must become a catcher. It was the reasoning of a twelve year old, and innumerable bruises, sore knees, jammed fingers, and passed balls could not convince me otherwise. Only the yearly cut from Little League, Pony League, or whatever league I was trying out for finally convinced me I was not going to be the second Clint Courtney. But I was hooked on Courtney, and I followed his less-than meteoric career as he bounced through baseball.

It was ten years after I saw him in the Durham uniform when I first met

2. Pack the Park

him in person as he came to Savannah to take over the managing job. He was great. After most games we would sit for hours in my office as Scraps held court with the media around a few six-packs of beer. One time I asked him about the green walnut story, to see if he really could throw a green walnut that far. Scraps remembered it and grinned broadly. "Hell, you can throw a green walnut further than anything. Why, if anybody hadda bet me, I'da taken all their money."

Courtney loved to bet if he had the odds, whether it was green walnuts, ping-pong, or a foot race. Once he bet the slowest catcher on our club to race around the bases. Scraps was then forty-five, and made the catcher take off one of his shoes, and with that advantage, Courtney won easily.

Scraps' fondness for beer has been well-documented. Pat Conroy, author of *The Great Santini* and *The Lords of Discipline*, came down to do a story on Courtney and wrote, "The beer can seems an extension of his thumb."

Scraps would stay in my apartment in Savannah before his family came up from Louisiana after school was out. The team trainer and I would share a "Scraps watch" after each game was over. It would be one of our responsibilities to go out drinking with Courtney to make certain he didn't get into too much trouble.

My main memory of those evenings was a night at a long-departed Savannah bar by the name of Mother's Pump Room. The bar was not one of the classier local watering spots, and one night as Scraps and I sat at the bar, a petite young thing decided fisticuffs were in order with a table of six Marines from nearby Parris Island. She was actually making headway through the leathernecks when someone pulled out a gun and cold-cocked her. As she was being dragged into the street, Scraps leaned over to me and said, "Miles, I like this place. We got to come here more often."

Fortunately, when the Courtney family would show up in early June, Scraps became a different person. The fights Courtney had with Billy Martin and others in baseball are legendary, but Dorothy Courtney, at 105 pounds, could handle Scraps better than any 300-pound bouncer. He would not dare cross his strong-willed wife.

It's probably not right to judge a man by his family, but the Courtney children were remarkable. His oldest boy, valedictorian in his high school, had been admitted to an accelerated pre-med program at Louisiana State and would enter med school in two years. Cindy, the oldest girl, was pretty and smart as a whip, but Scraps was most proud of her because she could lift three bales of hay at one time. The three youngest were all quiet and intelligent, and they would sit patiently outside the office as Scraps drank his beer after a ball game.

I often wondered how Clint Courtney, playing the role of country plowboy from Louisiana, could have such bright kids, but there were times when the other side of Courtney would slip out.

There's a Bulldozer on Home Plate

Al Gallagher played for Scraps in Richmond, and one day Al went into Courtney's hotel room without knocking. There, on the bed, was Scraps reading a thick history of World War II. Courtney was enraged, and he threatened Gallagher with dire consequences if he ever let it out that he had seen Scraps reading a book.

Scraps was managing Richmond when he died in 1975. The team was in Rochester, and after a game, Scraps was playing ping-pong in the motel with one of his players. At the age of 48, his heart gave out, and he was dead.

Gallagher, an over-the-hill ex–big-leaguer, had to take over as manager until the Braves could find someone to replace Scrap Iron. I was running the Jacksonville club then, and I flew to Louisiana on a hot, sweltering June day for the funeral. Gallagher had to stay with the Richmond club. He remembers it as the toughest thing he ever had to do, trying to convince his teammates they should play a ball game when no one wanted to, most of all Al. It was from that point that Al Gallagher decided he wanted to manage.

The last two years in Durham have been interesting for many reasons, but much of it was the sense of déjà vu as I watched Dirty Al manage. Many of his moves as a manager were pure Clint Courtney. There was pitcher Big Ike Pettaway playing third base so he could stay in the game to pitch to the next batter, and the intimidation of other teams with speed, learned from the Courtney classroom.

They say baseball is a game of memories. But with all that happens in baseball, I'm still surprised at my Courtney memories—how the images of the squatty little catcher still remain. But I can't complain. I wouldn't trade them for anything.

The season ended with the Savannah Braves just one game out of first place. Courtney managed the team to a near-championship, and enthusiasm for the team was growing. I was excited for the next season but also just excited to be in Savannah. It was a great city to be young, single, and full of ideas. With the new mayor, the city became alive, and it was no longer the sleepy Southern town known mainly for massive oaks, Spanish moss and historic homes. Outstanding restaurants and bars were opening, and River Street was becoming a nightly destination. It had become my town.

Nineteen seventy-three was the best season in Savannah. I now knew exactly what I wanted to do, and with Clint Courtney coming back as manager, the season was poised for great things. The Atlanta Braves with Hank Aaron played a spring training exhibition game at Grayson Stadium and drew 5,000 real fans. "Pack the Park" Opening Night remained one of the best promotions, and plans were in the works for other attendance-boosting events.

2. Pack the Park

The night following Opening Night had always proven to be one of the lowest attendance nights on the calendar. Pack the Park Night received all the publicity and we needed to give the second night a push. Plans were developed to make the second night special with a doubleheader scheduled and a giant fireworks extravaganza between games of the twin bill. The hope was that the fireworks would bring a crowd to rival Opening Night. "Extravaganza" might be a bit of a stretch with the budget for fireworks being $750, but the fireworks company promised the show would impress.

Getting a permit for the fireworks was not easy, and the paperwork for the permit needed to state at what time the fireworks would explode. The show was scheduled to start after the first game of the doubleheader, but baseball games have no clock and it was difficult to predict an exact time. On the permit I wrote 8:30 p.m., certain that the first game would be over by then. To shoot off the pyrotechnics, Savannah Beach's volunteer fire department members were enlisted. Perhaps there should have been a concern when I was informed that their fee was $50 and all the beer they could drink.

I believed that everything was planned to perfection for a great night, but unfortunately no plans had been made in the event the first game of the doubleheader went into extra innings. In the minor leagues, doubleheader games are scheduled for seven innings, and in this game, the score was tied at four after seven innings. Most extra-inning games need only a few innings more for the game to be decided, but this did not seem to be the case with this contest. As the evening wore on, a sinking feeling began churning in my stomach as little kids and their parents confronted me, asking when the fireworks would start. Finally, in the 17th inning around 11 p.m. with the score still tied at 4–4, I knew some type of action needed to take place. I pulled the umpires aside between innings and asked if the game could be delayed for about 15 minutes while the fireworks were shot off. The umpires would not budge. I was told the explosives could only be shot off whenever the game ended and not before.

By that point most of the crowd had left and it seemed pointless to have the display. I made the decision to cancel the event and shoot the fireworks off at a later date. Behind the outfield fence, the men of the Savannah Beach Volunteer Fire Department were feeling no pain, many hours of free beer having taken its toll. One sober soul remained, the chief, and he informed me that there was no way to re-crate the explosives and delay the display to another night. The evening moisture had

There's a Bulldozer on Home Plate

seeped inside the rockets, making the explosives dangerous. The fireworks would have to be shot off that night.

At midnight, I called the league office to see if there might be a 12 a.m. curfew so that the game could be postponed and the fireworks shot off. The league president informed me there was no curfew in the league and the contest must be completed. He did, however, give permission to postpone the second game of the doubleheader. That act of benevolence gave little comfort. Enough innings had been played to fill three games.

Finally, in the 23rd inning, Columbus scored six runs, and at 1 a.m. the game was over, Savannah losing, 10–4. The fireworks began. Standing at the top of the grandstand, I had to admit that $750 had bought a pretty good display. The only fans left in the park at that hour were the heavy drinkers, and after seven hours of free-flowing beer, they weren't quite certain what was happening. But with the bright display of lights high in the sky, a quartet of them locked arms and sang a boozy rendition of *The Star-Spangled Banner*.

I continued to watch and enjoy the display, with the only hesitation being that the fireworks seemed extremely loud. More than half of the rockets made just a brief flash, but ended in a huge BOOM. The fact that it was now Sunday morning played on my mind, for I knew most of the churchgoing citizens of Savannah would be long in bed. The display lasted close to 15 minutes, and when it was over, most of the drunks wobbled out. I wandered down to the office where I was met by 10 police officers. They were there to arrest me.

In the annals of Savannah police history, the night of April 14, 1973, was not one of the better evenings for the force. For 20 minutes between 1:00 and 1:20 a.m., the switchboard at the police barracks became completely overloaded. No calls could get through, and a squad of cars was dispatched to the ballpark. At radio and TV stations in the city, phones were clogged and nervous deejays were at a loss to tell listeners what was happening. The assistant city manager, a World War II veteran, was awakened by his wife, and as he listened to the reverberations, he assured his wife that the shelling was too far away to hit them, and she should go back to sleep.

Back at Grayson Stadium, I was doing some fast talking. I quickly pulled out our permits and licenses, showing the officers that everything was in order. Could they not have some sympathy? I had not planned for a 23-inning game. Fortunately, sympathy won out, and the police departed. By then, I was busy answering the phone as angry citizens, figuring out the source of the noise, began calling the ballpark.

2. Pack the Park

The language used should probably not be repeated. One man asked for my home phone so he could call at 4 a.m. to awaken me.

One positive comment did emerge from the otherwise negative reaction to the pyrotechnic display. An older lady who lived nearby wrote a note that she, too, had been awakened by the fireworks. In her closet she had been saving a bottle of gin for a special occasion, and she took this bottle with her to the front porch and polished it off as she sat and watched the fireworks. It was one of the best nights she had experienced in years, she wrote.

Except for the fireworks, everything was going smoothly in that third year. The situation changed in mid–May, when the Braves fired their manager in Richmond and called up Courtney to take over the Triple-A club. This was a shock. Scraps was replaced by Tommie Aaron, Hank's younger brother. Tommie had been sent to Savannah as a player-coach that season, and his transition to manager did not prove difficult. Scraps took two of Savannah's best pitchers with him to Richmond, but the team still did well and finished in second place, six and a half games out of first. Attendance increased, and the financials for the year were solid.

When I first had the dream of running a minor league team, it was not with the idea of making a career of baseball. I wanted to prove that minor league baseball could be successful and that the love of the game was possible to be transferred to others. After three years of running the Braves' farm team, I decided it was now time to

Clint Courtney, manager of the Savannah Braves, 1972–1973.

There's a Bulldozer on Home Plate

move on. Financially, the Braves' gamble on me had paid off, and Savannah was now a respectable minor league franchise. But I was a graduate of Johns Hopkins University and had received a master's degree from the University of Virginia. My thesis had been published and the publisher would like to see other efforts from me. Shouldn't I be looking for more? At the end of the third season, I wrote the Braves to let them know I was resigning. It was time to find something else.

3

Victoria, Toronto, Anderson and Others

That fall, I rented an apartment at Savannah Beach (now Tybee Island) for $110 a month and started work on the Great American Novel. But the novel did not come easily, and I struggled. In thoughts of possible other jobs, nothing materialized. Baseball was still part of my consciousness. That December I flew to baseball's Winter Meetings in Houston. I told myself it was just to see old friends and keep up contacts. But if the right opening developed, maybe I would take it.

The meetings were always great fun. Most years I went without hotel reservations, knowing someone would have an extra bed and let me crash with them. In Houston, I ran into an individual I had met only briefly at prior meetings. His name was Bob Freitas, and he would become my baseball guru. He was president of the Northwest League and the field representative for the National Association of Professional Baseball Leagues, the parent body of the minor leagues. For all these titles he did not make much more than $10,000 a year. He was a baseball lifer, a tall, soft-spoken, rumpled individual who had recently bought a laundromat to supplement his income.

Freitas knew I was without a club, and he drew me in as he introduced me to the joy of independent baseball. As president of the Northwest League, to keep his league alive, he had to convince several of his clubs to continue operating without a major league agreement. It was much more costly to run an independent club, having to pay the players and pay other expenses normally covered by the big-league parent club. Several cities in his league had operated independently to keep baseball alive with hope that a major league agreement would be available the following season.*

---

*In 1975, the *New Yorker* magazine published a long article on Freitas. The writer followed Freitas as he traveled from minor league city to minor league city in his job as the National Association field rep. He portrayed the difficulty of keeping minor league cities alive and Freitas's efforts to encourage these cities to stay in the game.

There's a Bulldozer on Home Plate

His message was one that captivated me. He pointed to the years of minor league baseball before Branch Rickey developed the farm system and to the period after World War II when many clubs did not have major league agreements. People came to the games to see their hometown team win. They did not care about the majors. However, financial considerations forced teams to fight for major league tie-ups, and those that didn't obtain an agreement died. The minors went from 58 leagues to 16. But Freitas kept his league alive without a full complement of major league working agreements, and in 1973 his message struck gold with the Portland (Ore.) Beavers.

The Beavers had been a Triple-A club in the Pacific Coast League for many years, but after the 1972 season, averaging just a little more than 1,000 fans a game, the team moved to Spokane. The territory was open and Freitas moved in to claim it for the Northwest League. Most baseball observers considered this folly. If a Triple-A club could not make it in that market, how could a team with a roster of mostly rookies, with a schedule of half the games, survive? But Freitas believed that an independent team might be able to succeed in the Portland market. He believed in his mantra of winning. He convinced Hollywood actor Bing Russell to come to Portland as the owner of the franchise. Russell, one of the larger-than-life characters one might meet a couple of times in a lifetime, brought new energy to the franchise. Major league baseball hated him.

For the next five years, the Portland Mavericks were the talk of baseball. Russell hired ex-big leaguers such as Jim Bouton and Luis Tiant to pitch. His manager Frank "The Flake" Peters was colorful and his goal was to win. The team averaged nearly 4,000 fans a game in most years. It was too much for the Pacific Coast League that needed a new city. Baseball rules allowed a team in a higher classification to draft a lower league, and at the end of the 1977 season, the Triple-A league drafted Portland. The Northwest League and Bing Russell were out. Despite high expectations, the new Portland teams averaged barely over 1,000 fans a game.*

Freitas sang the praises of Portland, and I was captivated. I loved running the Savannah Braves, but the job was not as satisfying as I had imagined. The Braves were a great organization to work for. They had given me the freedom to promote and operate the way I believed was

---

The Battered Bastards of Baseball is an outstanding documentary on Bing Russell and the Portland Mavericks.

3. Victoria, Toronto, Anderson and Others

best. They were good people, and I did not have the financial problems that many other minor league clubs experienced. But still, something was missing. The purpose of a minor league system for any major league club is not to win, but to develop the two or three players who might have the talent to make the big leagues.

I certainly understood that, but I also believed that winning was important. Most fans are not really excited to see a player learn to make a clean pivot on a double play. They come to root for the home team, and if the team's purpose isn't really to win, it becomes tough to get them to return. The good players are quickly moved to the next level, and it is difficult for fans to have allegiance to individual players. I looked at college sports where players weren't professional. The allegiance to these teams was remarkable in any sport, even if the university didn't have a winning record. Fans knew that the college players and coaches were always trying to win.

Freitas had me hooked and proposed that I try to put an independent team in Victoria, British Columbia. He praised the city and the ballpark. This was not on my radar when I came to the Winter Meetings. I needed to think about it. Once I was back in Savannah, the idea continued to grow, and within a week I called him. Without a lease on the ballpark or the funds to operate it, I still wanted to give it a try. Freitas let me know that the league was having a meeting in early January in Portland where the members would vote on expansion. Everything needed to be in order by the meeting. Within a few days I raised $10,000 from investors in Savannah to back efforts to start a club in a city 3,000 miles away in another country. Having once visited the city when in the Navy, I knew it was beautiful, but did the citizens want a baseball team? In my heart, I believed every city should want a baseball team, but, in truth, Victoria was a question mark. I packed my little decade-old VW with all my belongings and started the drive across the continent.

In Victoria, I started to meet with city fathers and local fans. The city did want a team, a lease was available, and the fans were there. The ballpark was also used for soccer, but that did not matter. It was a baseball park and I was anxious to start operations. The one formality was getting the franchise. I headed for the Northwest League meeting in Oregon to gain admission. The league was ready to expand by two teams from six to eight clubs, and at the meeting three groups, including myself, were present to make an application. I was confident in Victoria's chances. None of the other groups had any baseball management experience, and none of the cities had the population base of Victoria.

There's a Bulldozer on Home Plate

The success of Portland had created a new interest in the Northwest League. My goal was to operate a successful franchise. The other applicants had different goals. One applicant had a son-in-law he wanted to set up for a career in baseball management. His net worth was well over $1 million. The other prospective franchisee wanted a team so his son could play center field. His net worth was also over $1 million. The league directors looked at the other applicants' balance sheets and looked at my $10,000. This was a league that had barely survived for the last decade, and suddenly people with real money wanted to enter. The directors praised my experience, but it was not a contest. I started the long drive back to Savannah.

Bob Freitas was totally apologetic, but he did not need to be. I understood. He did not foresee the interest in his league. But it was the beginning of a long friendship. Every few months, he would send a letter on potential cities. He also began writing on cities that might make up a completely independent league, a league that could operate without major league interference. He believed that this should be the future of baseball. His dream became mine.

I was back at the beach, but it would not be for long. I had no phone, but the landlady who lived upstairs had let me use her number. She yelled from the apartment above to let me know there was a call for me. It was from an official with the Atlanta Braves asking if I would be interested in going to Toronto to work for a soccer club. My immediate reaction was "no." I didn't really know or like soccer and had just gotten out of sports to look for another career. But then he explained. A major league baseball franchise was expected to be granted to Toronto in the next couple of years, and he was part of a group applying for ownership. He needed someone on the ground in Toronto that knew baseball and would become part of that city. He felt it would be a great position to help lead baseball's entry into Toronto. I was intrigued and accepted the position.

The team I was to work with was the Toronto Metros, a new entry in the North American Soccer League. I arrived in early March. The club, owned by a lawyer, would be my first experience with a lawyer-owned sports team where an attorney with no knowledge becomes an immediate expert. My position was never terribly clear, but I started working, setting up for the season. I rented a room in a rooming house where the cooking odors mirrored the tastes of the Eastern European landlord. I was amazed at how clean and white a city Toronto was. I missed the grittiness of U.S. cities.

3. Victoria, Toronto, Anderson and Others

My mother had been sick with cancer, but she encouraged me to go. In early April she died, and I rushed back to North Carolina. When I returned to Toronto, there was an emptiness as I tried to become enthused about a soccer team. Hank Aaron was about to break Babe Ruth's home run record, and the potential record-breaking game was on national TV in the States. That night I went from bar to bar in Toronto trying to find a TV that might be broadcasting the baseball game. Every bar had only hockey for the patrons. Aaron broke the record that night, but I did not see it. I missed baseball, the U.S., and other things. This was not the job for me. I headed back to Georgia.

Back at the beach for less than a month, another phone call came on my landlady's line. This call was from one of the owners of the Anderson Mets in the Western Carolinas League. The season was underway, but things weren't going well for the franchise. The team needed to make a change at the GM position. Was I available? Available, yes, but did I want to go to Anderson, South Carolina? I was aware that this wasn't going to be a great situation. I asked the owner to give me 24 hours to decide.

Anderson could not be considered a booming city. It was part of an area in northwestern South Carolina that was growing. The population of Greenville, 30 miles to the north, was increasing and Clemson University, just 18 miles up the road, was an expanding major educational institution. Anderson's population was around 27,000, down from 40,000 in 1960. The city first received a WCL team in 1970 when a baseball hustler convinced the town to build a new ballpark seating around 3,000 fans. In the first year, the novelty of a new team captivated the city, and the announced attendance was 184,000, a figure that was difficult to believe. The owner appeared to work at alienating the city, and the next year attendance dropped to 50,000. In the following year, attendance was 29,000, fewer than 500 a game.

I decided to take the job and I made the call the next day. Nothing else was on the horizon, and I needed to be out of the beach apartment in a few weeks when the summer rentals started. Maybe I could help Anderson. After packing the car, I headed up.

Unfortunately, there was little I could do to resurrect the franchise. As with smaller towns, a hard core of a couple hundred fans was ready to do anything for the club. But much more was needed. Promotions and gimmicks were tried, but the numbers did not change. At one low point, I contemplated locking the gates and not admitting any fans. The proposal to ownership was to play the games at noon with no one in

There's a Bulldozer on Home Plate

Anderson, South Carolina. Anderson Memorial Stadium was built in 1970 as a home for a Western Carolinas League team. The team enjoyed immense success the first year, drawing more than 150,000 fans, but attendance quickly dropped off after the initial season and the team struggled to survive. The team left after the 1975 season. The Braves placed a team in the city from 1980 through 1984, but it also failed. An independent league placed a team in the city in 2007 with little success.

attendance. That would mean the club would no longer need ticket takers or sellers, ushers, or concession workers. There would be no need for a PA announcer or a cleanup crew and the franchise would have no electric bill for night games. Financially, the Anderson Mets might have been better off. The proposal was not accepted. For all the negatives, there was one good thing about that season, and that was Buford Lunsford.

Bulls Illustrated (July/August 1988)
A Season with the Anderson Mets

I had a call from Buford Lunsford a few weeks ago. I couldn't recall how long it had been since I last talked with him. It must have been at least five years, because he didn't know I was married and had two children. He was calling to see if I couldn't help his 16-year-old grandson get a real professional model glove. We talked about other things and mostly about a baseball season that for both of us was one of the worst but in many ways one of the best.

3. Victoria, Toronto, Anderson and Others

The first time I ever heard the name Buford Lunsford was in May of 1974 when he called me at Savannah Beach. I had moved back to the beach a month earlier, and since I didn't have a phone, my landlady came downstairs to tell me I had a call. On an extension that was out on the side porch, this polite, country voice introduced himself and inquired whether I might be interested in running the Anderson, South Carolina, club of the Single-A Western Carolinas League.

Eight months earlier, I had quit a Double-A Southern League GM's job with the intention of leaving baseball. I had spent three years in baseball, and now it was time to find a real job. But every job I explored had no appeal. Quite frankly, everything seemed to pale in comparison to running ball clubs.

I had taken a job with a soccer team in Toronto, but that hadn't worked out and I was back at the beach to sort things out. That was when the call came from Buford. The pay for the Anderson job was $600 a month, not great for a minor league G.M. with experience, but the season had already started and I was without a job. More than anything, I needed baseball. I packed my car and headed for Anderson.

I remember waiting at the Holiday Inn in Anderson (perhaps hiding would be a better word), because they had not yet told the old GM that he was fired. Buford had to do that task, and he delayed as much as possible. When I finally reported to the ballpark the next day, there were no keys because the former GM had refused to turn them over.

In 1974, the Anderson Mets were a terminal minor league franchise. It was the team's fifth year of existence, and the club had gone from being one of the glamour clubs of minor league baseball to the worst franchise in the game. In 1970 the city of Anderson, through donations and hard work, had built a new stadium so that the Shelby, N.C., club could move to Anderson. The city was tremendously proud of the accomplishment, and the town of 25,000 had drawn over 180,000 fans that first year. They were the talk of baseball, and the Atlanta Braves had even considered moving their Class AA club to the city because of the phenomenal attendance.

But the city had not paid attention to the individual they were getting as the owner of their new team. The bills started piling up, and payment on stadium construction and other items were delayed as the citizens tried to understand why payment would have to wait until next year. In the second season bills were still not paid and when the owner sneaked out of town with a month to go in the season, it was clear that another city had been raped by a minor league hustler. Anderson's love affair with minor league baseball quickly turned to hatred.

After that 1971 season, a group of local businessmen took over the franchise, hoping to salvage baseball for the city. But the damage was done and even local civic leaders could not erase the memory. It was the third year of

There's a Bulldozer on Home Plate

ownership by the local group when I arrived, and it was clear there was little enthusiasm for pumping more money into a moribund ball club.

Buford Lunsford had been named president of the Anderson Mets that third year. By then the more substantial local businessmen who had invested in the club didn't really want their names associated with the team, and Buford, who ran a little cabinet shop where he made kitchen and bathroom cabinets, took over the thankless job. Creditors from years back were still calling, and Buford, who was unfailingly polite and scrupulously honest, was probably the only individual who could have handled the task.

That season, in hopes of upgrading the operation, the club had gone out and hired a former assistant GM from Triple-A to run the operation. But it was the wrong choice, and by May, with no money coming in, they had to make a change. The minor league grapevine knew I was available, and I came to take over.

I'm pretty much of an optimist when it comes to running minor league clubs. I think baseball teams can make it in any town, but it wasn't long before I knew that the situation in Anderson was as close to hopeless as any I had seen. The current ownership—the official corporate name was Community Sports Inc.—had accumulated debts of close to $50,000, and although I thought the club might be able to reach a break-even situation, it could never wipe out that past debt.

Buford and I would meet each morning in his cabinet shop, and amid the sawdust and wood, we would talk over what bills we could pay or what we could do to get a little more money coming in. There wasn't much, but we hoped that something could happen to save the franchise.

Four months is not a terribly long time. That's how long I lived in Anderson. It is now some 14 years since I ran that club, but I have been left with some vivid memories. The fans that were left were extremely loyal. About 250 to 300 came every game, and they were dedicated to the players who had been sent to town by the New York Mets. The fan club had a collection of mattresses, kitchenware, and linens, and every player who came to town was given free use of everything he needed to furnish an apartment. Three or four older women acted as surrogate mothers for the players, and most nights they would bring me supper at the ballpark. Apparently, they were under the impression that a diet of hot dogs and cokes was not terribly healthy, and so at night I would be brought fried chicken and potato salad and green beans and iced tea.

The Mets, who were our parent club, tried to help out, and one weekend they sent us Willie Mays to give the team a little publicity. Willie was listed as an instructor in their farm system, but he was not interested in doing anything to promote the club. A photo in the local paper showed Buford Lunsford squatting down beside Willie who was sitting in a chair behind the clubhouse. Buford was begging Willie to at least come out and wave to the crowd

3. Victoria, Toronto, Anderson and Others

instead of hiding behind the clubhouse in right field. Willie refused—he wasn't going to accommodate anyone—and the club, which had spent money it didn't have to advertise his appearance, gained only more unhappy fans from Willie's non-appearance.

By August we knew nothing was going to help the club. The team was fifth in a six-team league and would end up some 23 games out of first place. The only prospect was an 18-year-old phenom named Lee Mazzilli. The field manager was uncooperative and dealings with the club on the field were strained most of the time. That month we ran out of money. I stopped paying myself, and we had to let go of most of the part-time employees. I still remember getting up at 6 a.m. to clean the stadium because we did not have enough money to pay the cleanup man.

After the season, we had a meeting of the stockholders. Buford and I told them the inevitable. The only thing to do was fold the team. There was no money, three years' worth of debts, and prospects for the future were non-existent. I stuck around town a week or so more until the final reimbursement check came from the Mets and I could pay myself the final few paychecks. Buford and I collected the few assets of the franchise: a tractor, some uniforms, and rakes, and stored them in the cellar of his cabinet shop. That was it.

If it had been 10 years or so later, the franchise might have been worth something. The corporation could have sold the team to clear the debts and perhaps make a little money. But in the early 1970's minor league franchises had no value, and no one wanted to take over something that was almost sure to lose money. It was not the absolute end of professional baseball in Anderson. The following year the Gastonia club moved to Anderson, but that team lasted only one year before packing its bags and moving on to Asheville. In 1980 the Braves moved the Greenwood club to Anderson for a few years. But the city was doomed for baseball because of too little population and an operator who ran off with the money.

Buford and I talked mostly about 1974. There were a lot of memories, but for me, the best part of that year was a friendship with Buford Lunsford, one of the most polite and honorable men I've ever met. Tough times are often more memorable, and friendships made in adversity a little more meaningful. Buford and I had a little catching up to do. He had a heart attack a few years back and one of his sons had taken over the cabinet shop. He still worked a good part of the day at the store, but his pace was a bit slower.

I wouldn't want to go back and run an Anderson, S.C., ball club again, but it isn't bad to have an Anderson in your background as well as a Durham. And it is good to know that there will be decent people along the way. I'll be getting that glove for Buford's grandson.

4

Jacksonville, Richmond, Vancouver and Victoria

In trying to recall my thoughts on the future, it is difficult to recall what the final goal was at this time. I still had the baseball dream of an independent club, but that was not progressing. I was midway through writing my *Cockatrice* trilogy, but it was going slowly and publishers seemed little interested in the tale of a drunk, mythical serpent able to kill with a glance. In one of my nightly trips to a favored Savannah watering hole, Jim Collins' or Eddie Pasco's place, I sat next to a well-dressed older businessman who began giving advice on my future. His message was that if one is not on the road to be head of a major business by the age of 35, he will never succeed in life. Approaching that age myself, it was difficult to say that I was on the road, much less a path, to anything. For a day or so, I was a bit depressed about the future, but then as I mulled it over, I wasn't certain I wanted to be on a specific road. The truth was I liked my current life. With no final goal in mind, I was content to let the path lead to wherever it might go.

In late spring, another call came. This time the call was to take over as general manager of the Jacksonville Suns in the Double-A Southern League. The current GM had just accepted a position as head of the Jacksonville Express, a team in the newly-formed World Football League. Suns ownership was desperate for an experienced GM to be the replacement. With few unemployed, experienced minor league GMs available in the middle of a baseball season, I became the only choice. As in the prior year, with money short and beach housing about to be unavailable, I quickly accepted.

In many ways, Jacksonville, Florida, was the opposite of Anderson. Jacksonville was a major city with a strong baseball history. Wolfson Stadium, a quality facility, was more than double the size of Anderson Memorial Stadium, and the Southern League level of baseball was considerably better than the mostly-rookie Western Carolinas League.

4. Jacksonville, Richmond, Vancouver and Victoria

Jacksonville, Florida. Sam Wolfson Park was for many years the home of minor league baseball in Jacksonville. The facility was completed in the mid–1950s and teams from the South Atlantic League, International League, and Southern League competed in the facility until a new park opened in 2003.

Unfortunately, there were a couple of similarities. The team was a strong candidate for last place and the attendance was usually in the hundreds, not thousands.

The team was a farm club of the Kansas City Royals. The organization was not filled with great prospects at that time, and the Jacksonville club struggled. The Royals had sent as manager a 34-year-old former minor league outfielder named Billy Scripture. While he was engaging and personable, Billy was also a bit different, and he made the summer in Jacksonville totally memorable.

Bulls Illustrated (April/May 1986)
Memories from a Beer Can

I was cleaning out my closet the other day when I came across an old beer can. I do have some fond memories of beer cans, but normally I don't save them. But this one was special and brings back memories of 1975 in Jacksonville, Fla. First, the beer can needs some explanation. It is a 12-ounce Miller can, and there is nothing particularly different about it—except there is a

There's a Bulldozer on Home Plate

huge hole in the side of it. The hole was put there by the field manager. He was able to make the hole by eating the side out of that beer can. I always thought that was a pretty unique trick, but then Billy Scripture, manager of the 1975 Jacksonville Suns, was a pretty unique manager.

The thing about Billy was that he had great teeth. I had never seen him as a player, but there were stories that in a tense situation during a game, he would get down on his knees and start chewing the side of a dugout bench. He once told me that he would chew on rocks to calm himself. Billy was a graduate of Wake Forest University, but he was not your normal, sedate graduate of that prestigious Baptist institution. Once, while playing for Rochester, he was thrown out of a game. Rather than go to the clubhouse, he climbed a light tower and watched the rest of the game from there.

Now, I'm not certain how many of the Billy Scripture stories I heard were true, but I can vouch for his teeth. As with any good players, as they get older the skills diminish. Billy was in his mid-thirties when we first met, and his teeth had slowed a bit. He certainly no longer chewed dugout benches. But one day he was talking and told me he could eat a baseball.

Early in my baseball career, I learned not to doubt what a manager told me. They were the baseball experts, and common sense dictated that it was best to believe your manager. But my mother also hadn't raised a fool, and my skepticism over Billy's ability to eat baseballs must have shown. Billy kept insisting he could do it, and in the next few days we set up a demonstration. One of the local sportswriters heard about it, and he brought along a photographer. Sure enough, Billy ate a baseball. Well, to be truthful, it wasn't as much eating as ripping a baseball apart with his teeth. Then, to top it off, Billy ate the side out of a beer can. I saved the can.

The photo of Billy eating the baseball made the national wire. In a few days we had a call from NBC and Joe Garagiola. Joe wanted Billy for his Baseball World show. Joe and the NBC crew came down, and Billy did a few of his other tricks for national TV. One of his best was breaking a wood bat with his bare hands. He also stood in front of a pitching machine running at top speed and let the balls bounce off his chest. For his grand finale, he ate a baseball.

Unfortunately, Billy's abilities that year did not extend to managing, and the team ended up in last place, 22 games out of first. At one point, Billy took a couple of days off to go skeet shooting without telling anyone but an assistant coach. The Kansas City Royals were not happy.

There were a few interesting, if not talented, players on that club. One was a mortician in the off season. His name was Pickle. Another player had once beaten a VW bug in a 100-yard dash, but that was a skill seldom needed on a baseball field. A few of the players made the big leagues and had decent careers. Late in the season, the Royals sent a pitcher, a non-prospect undrafted free agent, to fill out the roster. Nothing much was expected of him, but ultimately Dan Quisenberry had an outstanding big-league career.

4. Jacksonville, Richmond, Vancouver and Victoria

It was one of those seasons when nothing seemed to go right. Late in August, a thunderstorm blew through the city, and one of our outfield light towers was toppled over. We played the rest of the season with the right field in near darkness. One Sunday afternoon, we took in the smallest amount of money at the gate that I've ever seen in minor league baseball. The take was $42. The owners were not pleased.

At the end of the season, there was no question that I didn't want to return for another year. I turned in my resignation. As I recall, the owners did not try to talk me into staying. Jacksonville is a great city, but it wasn't my town. I headed back to Savannah Beach.

That fall, I watched the World Series on a little black and white TV. Since becoming involved in minor league baseball I had not followed the big leagues closely. However, the series captured me, and the intensity with the home runs by Bernie Carbo and Carlton Fisk brought back some of the special joys of baseball. I remembered why I loved the game. It was good to get a reminder. It also reminded much of the country about the joys of baseball. A resurgence of baseball interest across the U.S. happened in the next few years.

In 1976 there were no phone calls for jobs, but I was able to keep the beach place over the summer. For income, I worked part-time jobs for the Savannah Braves as the official scorer or public address announcer. I continued to try to write. My mother had left me a few stocks, and the modest dividends from these kept me in groceries. Late in '76 a

Jacksonville Suns manager Billy Scripture chewing on a baseball in 1975. Scripture's masticatory talents also included chewing the side out of a beer can and gnawing on rocks.

There's a Bulldozer on Home Plate

friend called. He asked if I would come to Richmond, Virginia, as the play-by-play broadcaster for the 1977 season. Richmond was a Triple-A club in the International League, a farm club of the Atlanta Braves. My friend had just been named the GM, but he had never run a club at that level. He really wanted my help in the front office, but his budget would only allow him to hire a play-by-play announcer. I took the job as front office assistant and play-by-play man and headed up to Richmond.

Baseball is a game for the senses. One can hear the crack of the bat, the cheers of the crowd, the cries of the vendors peddling peanuts and beer. The eyes see the green grass, the streaming rays of the lights from the towers spilling on the field, and the human reactions—joy, anger, despair—of spectators to the action on the field. Memory brings back the sweet smell of leather and your first glove. On entering the stadium, the smell of popcorn popping and hot dogs roasting brings memories of your first hot dog at a ball game. And if one can get close enough to the field, there is the smell of fresh cut grass. Each ballpark has its unique smell. In Durham, when tobacco was a dying king, the fresh, sweet smell of tobacco leaves spilled over the stadium. In Amarillo the stockyards provide an odor that, while not always pleasing, informed spectators that Amarillo was a western cattle town. And in Richmond, one could smell cookies being baked. It was a grand odor. A cookie factory was near Parker Field, and it made for one of the most delightful ballpark smells imaginable.

I arrived in Richmond in early January as the staff began preparations for the season. The living arrangements were a rusting mobile home situated inside the ballpark down the right field foul corner. Three of the staff, including myself, made this home. It was not unpleasant to live at the stadium, even in an old trailer that had seen better days. Parker Field had been home for Richmond baseball since 1953 when Triple-A baseball moved to the city. The location had originally been a race track of some sort, and to make it usable for baseball, an old grandstand was moved from Scranton, Pennsylvania, when that city lost its team. The facility was a bit ramshackle, but it smelled like baseball (and cookies). I was part of the efforts to get everything ready for the season, and when the season started, it was time to take the role of play-by-play man.

I had been the broadcaster for Johns Hopkins football and lacrosse and had done some baseball in Savannah, filling in for the regular announcer. Having never done a full season of baseball, I looked

4. Jacksonville, Richmond, Vancouver and Victoria

forward to the job with a bit of nervousness. The press box in Richmond, which included a small, one-person partition for radio, was attached high under the roof of the Richmond stadium. I would have to be play-by-play man, color man, and engineer all rolled into one. Nothing was in the budget for a second person, although for some home games an unpaid local college student who was studying broadcasting filled in for a couple of innings. (Twenty years later I would run into him in Sioux Falls where he was the city's leading sports broadcaster.) On the road, I carried all the out-of-date equipment in a bulky suitcase. As I traveled by air to most road games, it proved difficult to find room on the small planes to store the heavy equipment box. Visiting radio booths in the International League were not much better than the space in Richmond, and one snowy April evening in Syracuse with no window to protect from the elements, the snow blew in, covering my score sheet and subjecting me to a cold that lingered for a month.

As I was a one-man show, I had no one to back me up if a play was missed. In a game in Columbus, Ohio, the home team executed a triple play. Regrettably, I had taken my eyes off the field for just a moment, and when I looked back to see the teams changing sides, I had no clue what had happened. My fumbling as I regrouped was not quality radio. Several older female fans commented that they liked listening to me before they went to bed because the broadcasts help put them to sleep. I was not certain that this was a compliment.

The International League season was 140 games long with only four off days from April 15 to September 4. The Richmond Braves made the playoffs which added four more games, but the team failed to make it to the finals. After the team's elimination, I received a phone call from the Charleston, West Virginia, team's broadcaster who asked if I could fill in for him in the championship finals. He had a college football gig that was starting and could not finish the season for Charleston. There was no hesitation when I told him "no."

I don't ever remember being so tired at season's end as that year in Richmond. In the GM role, I always thought the radio guy had it easy. He simply had to watch a baseball game for two or three hours and tell the audience what was happening. I did not appreciate the grind of a baseball season with seven games a week and long travel. The broadcaster had to compile all statistics for both teams because, in that era, there were no statistics companies that sent daily stats. He had to arrange for a pre-game interview and a post-game scoreboard show. And certainly as a GM, I never appreciated how tough it was on the players who have it much rougher than the broadcaster. Play-by-play opened my eyes to another facet of the minor leagues.

The season also opened my eyes to what I wanted to do in baseball. Broadcasting was not part of the plan. The International League had some play-by-play men with major league-level talent calling the games, but after many years, these professionals were still stuck at Triple-A. Former players or local personalities were often hired to be major league broadcasters, and many great broadcasters in the minors never got the shot. If I was going to be in baseball, it was in the front office.

There are good memories of Richmond. I loved the smell of the cookie factory. A bar downtown was a favorite. It was run by a British gentleman, and one of the patrons, if encouraged by enough Scottish malt, would bring out his bagpipe and fill the small establishment with mournful Scottish melodies. The staff in Richmond was great, and the team had outstanding players, 22 of whom would play in the big leagues. But the best memories are of the manager, Tommie Aaron.

Bulls Illustrated (July/August 1983)
My Friend Tommie Aaron

I guess I haven't seen Tommie Aaron for three or four years now, and although I might send a Christmas card every other year, I haven't kept in touch. But I've been thinking of Tommie lately.

Back in May, Sonny Jackson, who was a coach for the Bulls, had to leave quickly to join the Atlanta Braves to be their first base coach. Tommie, the regular first base coach, had gone back into the hospital. For the past year Tommie had been in and out of the hospital because of a blood disorder, and with the vague reports filtering out of Atlanta, I just hope things are going well for him.

I first met Tommie back in 1973 when I was general manager of the Savannah Braves and Tommie was sent there as the player-coach. I knew he was Hank Aaron's brother, and Hank was then starting to close in on Babe Ruth's home run record, but the word throughout the Atlanta minor league system on Tommie was all good.

By 1973, Tommie had been playing professionally for fourteen years since signing out of high school in Mobile, Ala. He had some time in the big leagues, but most of his career had been spent in Triple-A. He had some really outstanding years and could play first base, third base, and the outfield. Many people wondered why he didn't spend more time in the big leagues.

In his last few years as a player, Tommie (or "T-Bone," as he is known around the clubhouse) was being groomed as a manager. When he was sent to

4. Jacksonville, Richmond, Vancouver and Victoria

Savannah, it was the first official sign that the Braves were looking at him as something more than a player.

The Savannah manager that year was Clint "Scrap Iron" Courtney, and as much as Scraps might have liked to have Tommie sitting on the bench, soaking up coaching knowledge, Scraps more wanted to win. In Tommie Aaron, he had a winner, and so throughout April and May for every inning of every game, Coach Tommie Aaron was playing first base. There was the memorable 23-inning game that Tommie played throughout, and he still holds the Southern League record for most chances accepted by a first baseman in one game (33).

All that changed in late May. The Richmond Triple-A club was going through a terrible slump, and their manager was fired. The next day in Savannah we received a call that Courtney was to report to Richmond immediately as manager. Eddie Haas, one of the outstanding baseball men in the Braves organization, was to replace Scraps in Savannah.

It was a good thing the game that night was rained out, because Scraps started pounding the beer in mid-afternoon and began muttering that Atlanta should promote "HIS" coach to be the new Savannah manager. He was talking about Tommie.

As the news of the Courtney promotion filtered through the town, the sports editor of the newspaper, Marcus Holland, and the city's chief baseball backer, Judge Julius Fine, came to my office and listened as Scraps argued that Tommie Aaron should be the next Savannah manager.

Anybody who has ever worked with a major league club, and particularly the Braves, knows that the decisions are made at the major league level and input from the minor league side is neither welcomed nor encouraged.

But Scraps kept talking, and before long he had both the sports editor and Judge Fine on the phone to Atlanta demanding that Tommie be named to replace Courtney. By this time, Tommie had also come to the office, and I think he was enjoying the commotion that Scraps was causing. I looked over at him and asked how he felt about being manager, fully expecting Tommie to say he was happy being a coach. But Tommie surprised me by saying he'd like to give the Savannah job a try.

It was not long after that that I phoned Atlanta and told the farm director it might be good if Tommie Aaron could be named the new Savannah manager.

It is difficult to recall now why I did that, for Eddie Haas, the man scheduled to come to Savannah, had broken me into baseball and was outstanding. And Atlanta certainly wasn't asking me for my opinion. The farm director said he'd think about it.

We all sat around the office until early evening, waiting for the final decision, and near suppertime the call came. Tommie Aaron was the new Savannah manager.

There's a Bulldozer on Home Plate

It is important to put this in some perspective. The year was 1973, and before that year there had been only one African American manager in the history of either the major or minor leagues.*

Savannah is part of the old South. It is a city of tradition where the old ways die hard. Segregation had been part of the old ways, and in 1962 the Savannah minor league club moved to Lynchburg, Va., in mid-season rather than meet demands that the club integrate seating for spectators. The official who made the announcement to the fans that the club was moving was Judge Julius Fine. But with Tommie, race never seemed to be a factor.

I don't remember that much about the rest of the season. Scraps took the two best pitchers with him to Richmond, and for a while, Savannah struggled. Tommie would always come into the office after the game for a beer, and it was interesting to see him make the transition from player to manager.

At first, he continued to play first base, but as the season progressed, he put himself in the lineup fewer and fewer times. He began reacting like a manager, and as with others in his position, bases on balls would drive him up the wall.

Tommie spent the next four years managing the Savannah club while my next four years were spent in a half dozen jobs, knocking around from town to town. But Savannah had become home by then, and whenever another of my ventures fell flat, I'd move back to Savannah and stop by the ballpark and have a beer with Tommie.

By 1977 Tommie Aaron was promoted to manager of the Triple-A Richmond Braves, and that year I managed to hook on with Richmond as the play-by-play broadcaster. It was enjoyable being with Tommie, and although I found out I wasn't going to make a career of play-by-play, it was a good year.

One of the unwritten rules of baseball is that a manager doesn't drink with his players, so after the away games, it was Tommie and I and occasionally pitching coach Wes Westrum going down to the hotel bar to unwind with a couple of beers. Tommie didn't carry a loss for long, and although he would shake his head over the play of some of his team, he, for the most part, was remarkably good-humored. He had a great grin and a good laugh, and the time after the games was a great way for me to learn a little baseball.

Sitting in a bar as a radio announcer having a drink with your manager is not so unusual, but I used to think about it at times because of the difference in our race. I grew up in the South during the time of segregation, back of the bus, white and colored drinking fountains, and all those other laws that seem so perverse now. But they were effective, and by the time I got into baseball in the early seventies, I had never really known a black person.

---

*Former Chicago Cubs and Pittsburgh Pirates infielder Gene Baker managed Batavia, N.Y., in the New York–Penn League in 1961 and 1964. Frank Robinson became manager of the Cleveland Indians in 1975. There also had been African American managers in the Mexican and Provincial Leagues.

4. Jacksonville, Richmond, Vancouver and Victoria

I'm not particularly comfortable talking about race, but baseball has been a good education in this area. In an imperfect world, baseball may have it on a lot of other professions, for ultimately you are judged on your batting average or how hard you throw and how you produce, rather than family or money or color of skin.

The good memories filter back from those years with Tommie. We would sit in the clubhouse in Richmond with a paper sack full of steamed crabs—Tommie, Wes, and I—cracking them open and eating them after a game. Or the early morning team bus rides to Washington National Airport, where we would sit in the coffee shop, chatting and waiting for the plane to Pawtucket.

I'm not sure what constitutes an old friendship when you don't see the individual anymore. Sometimes there are just vague memories and no real desire to keep up with the person. But the memories of Tommie are good, and it would be a fine thing to sit down with him again over a beer and some steamed crabs. I hope he is well soon.

(Tommie Aaron died August 16, 1984.)

I was back at the beach. My publisher had given encouragement on a manuscript but did not believe it was yet publishable. Was I wasting time writing? If baseball was to be my career, it was time to get serious about that profession. I was 34 and in the last four years no baseball job that lasted more than six months. My credibility in the game was declining. Baseball people were aware of the jumping from job to job. It was time to find something permanent.

I made some phone calls and wrote letters that fall, but nothing was developing. The best place to look for a job in baseball was always the Winter Meetings. However, in the winter of 1977 the meetings were in Hawaii, and there was no way to afford that trip. So, it was a surprise when I received a phone call one evening from Hawaii. The president of the Carolina League, Jim Mills, was on the line, and he proudly told me that I had been awarded the Kinston, North Carolina, franchise in the league. I was more than slightly surprised. I had not put in an application for the team and had only been to the city once in my life. More importantly, I did not have the money to start a franchise from scratch. Jim Mills told me not to worry about the money. A former owner of the Atlanta Braves who knew me from Savannah was willing to be the principal backer.

At that time the Carolina League was struggling to survive. It was a Single-A league that in the 1960s had grown to as many as 12 franchises. However, major league teams cut back on farm teams in the 1970s, and by 1977, the Carolina League had only four teams. The league was about

There's a Bulldozer on Home Plate

to fold when Jim Mills, taking a page from Bob Freitas of the Northwest League, decided to add two independent clubs in 1978. At the winter meetings he announced to the baseball establishment that the league was expanding to six teams and that Miles Wolff would own Kinston and a Virginia businessman would own the team in Alexandria, Virginia. Both clubs were to be independent. Jim knew of my interest in independent baseball and believed I would be willing to go along with the plan.

When Jim told me that he had a backer, it took little time to become excited about the possibility. This could be my independent franchise. Within the week, I packed the car and headed to Kinston. Checking into a small motel, I began meeting people and assessing the city's potential. Kinston has a long history in professional baseball. In 1937 the city was one of the charter members of the Class D Coastal Plain League and in the 1960s had been one of the most successful franchises in the Carolina League. But excitement for baseball had worn off, and the team left the city in 1974. Kinston was not a large city—its population was around 25,000—and had not grown in recent years.

I had not yet talked with the potential backer, as Jim Mills had delayed giving me the phone number. When I finally reached the backer, he asked me the most important question: "Can we make money in Kinston?" I was honest with him. I told him that if it were an affiliated team, the franchise could possibly break even. However, it would take another $100,000 or more to subsidize an independent club. Kinston was too small a market. My backer, a very good businessman, was no longer interested. I called Jim Mills, let him know the situation, and departed Kinston. Fortunately for the Carolina League, Jim was able to find someone else who could operate a club and risk the losses. Kinston did become a member of the league in 1978 as an independent team.

Again back at the beach, wondering what direction to take, I received another phone call. On the line was a long-time minor league baseball executive who was helping a first-time owner set up a new Triple-A club in Vancouver, B.C. Would I be interested in coming to Vancouver? This was interesting. To be on the ground floor of a new club in a major city was intriguing. The team needed someone right away and he asked if I could fly out. Details were vague, but I was under the impression that the job being offered was that of GM. I booked a flight and was on my way to Canada.

Vancouver was a beautiful city, and the ballpark, while an older structure, had character and a real baseball feel. The owner was an

4. Jacksonville, Richmond, Vancouver and Victoria

individual named Harry Ornest. In later years, Harry would own the St. Louis Blues of the National Hockey League and the Toronto Argonauts of the Canadian Football League. He and his wife, Ruthie, were hands-on owners, and they directed every aspect of the operation. It was a difficult situation. The couple were not looking for any advice or suggestions, and my role was that of a hired hand. I lasted one week. I went to Harry and let him know it wasn't going to work. If he would pay for the airfare back to Savannah, I would need no other compensation. The deal was done and I was gone.

Before leaving British Columbia, I took the ferry over to Victoria. In 1974 I had tried to put a club in the city and I wanted to see if there was still interest. Again I met with local baseball people who were still enthusiastic about the possibility. The town was ready for a team. Although it was late to be trying to set up a team, I contacted the Northwest League to see if something could be done. The league still had strong interest in expanding to that city but needed another club to pair with Victoria. League officials felt it would be a long-shot to find another city and also an owner willing to subsidize a team. It made no sense for me to wait around to see if another team might be ready. I took my plane ticket and headed back to Savannah.

A week later the message came. The Northwest League had found a city to pair with Victoria, and the league was going to expand. Unfortunately, another group had made an application for Victoria and that group was being awarded the franchise. I was out of luck. Kinston, Vancouver, and Victoria had all fallen through in just a few months' time, and I was without a job in the game. I tried to reassess what I was doing. The writing had produced nothing, and baseball was at a dead end. It was not a time of positive thinking.

Fortunately, it was difficult to stay depressed in Savannah for long. And that might have been part of the problem. The appeal of the city was strong, and although financially things were tight, everything else about the lifestyle was positive. I lived in a beachfront house with minimal rent. Every morning a run on the beach started the day, and it was rare, even in winter, for the temperature to drop low enough that a little space heater was needed to warm the apartment. I had good friends to go crabbing with, and bartenders at favorite drinking establishments would pass a free beer now and then. On occasion a young lady might help to warm the apartment, and the city itself was a beautiful and historic place to explore. Did I ever want to leave?

I had gained a good reputation running the Savannah Braves, but it was years since I had done anything significant in the game. I was this guy who was always available but never stayed more than a year. I had quit the Savannah Braves with the idea of finding another profession but had never found it. I was trying to write but had published nothing since 1970. It was 1979, and there was a need to get serious. The only thing I knew and the profession I loved was running minor league clubs. But working for someone else was rarely satisfying. I knew the business and knew I could be successful. It was time to own my own team.

It was a great time to be looking to own a minor league franchise. Most believed minor league teams had no value and prices were minimal. Few people outside the game were looking to own ball clubs. At the winter meetings a longtime owner of clubs was offering to sell his teams in Gastonia and Pittsfield. I expressed interest in Gastonia, and he asked for $4,000 for the franchise. I countered with $1,000, saying that the only assets he had were a tractor and some uniforms. We never found a compromise price. He was unable to sell either club, and in desperation, he took an ad in the *Wall Street Journal* classifieds and offered Pittsfield for $40,000. Among minor league owners, there was shock and amazement when he found a buyer at that price. From that point on, the value of franchises started to rise as those outside the game began to see value.

Several minor leagues were looking to expand for 1980, and the Southern League and the Carolina League appeared to be the best bets to pursue. Macon, Georgia, was a promising possibility in the Southern League. The Macon Peaches held a strong history in minor league baseball, and without a team for the last decade, the town was poised for the return of baseball. In the Carolina League, Durham appeared as a possibility for a new franchise. But the league needed two cities to expand, and few other municipalities were interested.

In the short term in the spring of 1979, I took a six-week job with the Atlanta Braves at their minor league spring training complex in West Palm Beach, Florida. My job was to organize contracts, meal money, and payroll for about 120 Braves' farm players who were in camp trying to make a team. It was a good experience to learn another aspect of professional baseball, and it was my first contact with one of the Braves' minor league managers, "Dirty Al" Gallagher. He would be important in the next few years.

Upon returning to Savannah after spring training, my efforts started with the purpose of acquiring a club. The first and best hope was Macon. Along with Birmingham, Alabama, these two cities were

4. Jacksonville, Richmond, Vancouver and Victoria

traditional Southern League members and the league was eager to welcome them into the fold. Unfortunately, the National Association ruled that the two Double-A expansion cities had to go to the Eastern League. The Double-A leagues were expanding because the American League had added Toronto and Seattle in 1977. Now those major league teams needed Double-A affiliates. The Southern League had 10 teams and the Eastern League had six, and the minor league head office wanted to strengthen the Eastern by adding the teams to that league. The Eastern added Glens Falls, New York, and Lynn, Massachusetts, two marginal markets that ultimately failed. Macon was now out of the picture.

Durham then became the focus. One of the leading owners and operators in minor league baseball had been in Durham prior to my efforts. He was the Carolina League's leading candidate for the new franchise, but in a tour of Durham Athletic Park (the DAP) with city officials, he announced that the only way that Durham would ever get baseball was to blow up the old stadium and build a new facility. Reportedly, a rat had run across his foot in the tour which added to the negativity he saw in the old ballpark.

In my tour, I could recognize why he felt the ballpark was unsatisfactory for professional baseball. No pro team had played in the facility since 1971. Built in 1939 after a fire destroyed the original park, the field and the grandstand were in shambles. Little grass remained on the infield, and a rodeo had been held in the outfield, leaving huge divots. Lighting was poor and the outfield fence had been torn down. The grandstand seating was bleachers with no backs, and restrooms and concession areas were inadequate. Parking was extremely limited. Yet, I fell in love with the DAP. I loved old ballparks and this one could be fixed up. The city of Durham was willing to help. I knew I could make it in this park if the franchise came my way.

Several other groups were pursuing the franchise, but I had one big advantage. The Atlanta Braves wanted to put a team in the Carolina League, and they were willing to work with me. Previously, the Braves had only four farm teams. The organization had experienced difficulties with local ownership, and as a result, it owned these teams. Fortunately for me, the Braves did not want to own the Carolina League club and felt comfortable with my knowledge of their systems. And the league, needing an eighth team, had an operator willing to put an independent team in Rocky Mount, North Carolina. By September, everything was in order. I became owner of the Durham Bulls. The name had been part of Durham's baseball history, and I was not about to change

There's a Bulldozer on Home Plate

Durham Athletic Park. Durham (N.C.) Athletic Park was the home of the Durham Bulls from its construction in 1939 to 1995 when the new Durham Bulls Athletic Park was completed. The site was the home for the Bulls starting in 1926 when a new wooden park, El Toro Park, was completed. That park burned down in June 1939 and the concrete and steel facility was completed for the 1940 season. The movie *Bull Durham* was filmed at the facility. Miles Wolff was owner of the Bulls from 1980 to 1991.

4. Jacksonville, Richmond, Vancouver and Victoria

it. Bull Durham smoking tobacco had been the nation's largest selling smoking tobacco at the turn of the 20th century when the first professional team in Durham was named.

It was fall when I returned to Savannah to pack up my belongings. Savannah had been a great ten years. The town had always welcomed me back when things didn't work out. The beauty and atmosphere of the city captured me, but it was time to make the complete break.

Savannah 1979

Savannah: even the name fits. It is the name of an older woman who has not forgotten, who remembers when she was young, and she holds young men until their youth is spent. How did she keep you? What made you stay so long? And now that you are leaving, why does she still have this hold on you?

She is old—too old—with her ancient houses, and squares, and streets, preserved as a reminder of her youth. A man can wander and walk her streets and sit on her benches and never think about the miles of unpaved alleys, and rickety shacks, and old Black men standing on corners with nothing to do. The river is her necklace with glittering ships heading to seas, and you can stand and think about adventure with vessels going to faraway places. The bars are nearby, and the bartenders know your name and call you to drink their liquids, and you mellow out while you sip and stare as the ships and time pass by.

And there are the daughters of Savannah. She uses them well. She puts them in the apartments in the old houses on the old streets, and she has them lure the young men to stay a little longer. On the third floor of the big townhouse on the square she placed the girl with the laughing eyes. The laughing eyes would fix spaghetti and serve it sitting cross-legged on the big Oriental rug because there wasn't enough money for furniture, only for the Oriental rug. And then afterwards the only thing to do was lie on the rug and stare into the laughing eyes. There was the schoolteacher who lived in the back apartment of the old mansion on the corner. She was intelligent, alive, and then it was over. Did I leave first? Did she? Why did these things always drift into nothingness when they could have lasted forever? There was the blue blood with the poodle, and the girl in the carriage house and the barmaids on the waterfront who would slip you drinks. They were all part of Savannah's plan, making you stay a little longer when you should have left much earlier.

The attraction, what was the attraction? The weather? The climate? Could it have been worse? The summers were unbearable ... hot, muggy, with afternoon showers to make steam rise from black asphalt, soaking clothes with perspiration and matting the hair with sweat. The dusty, unpaved streets would turn to mud, filling their ruts with a thick, brown, splashing liquid. And at night, the same humid, oppressiveness made bodies stick together,

There's a Bulldozer on Home Plate

made physical efforts turn to the sweaty, slippery noise of flesh on flesh. When it was over, there was only quiet panting with bodies uncovered, hoping for any breeze through an open window to dry skin and make sleep accessible.

The winter—God, how miserable the winters could be. Savannah's flacks would say it is a temperate winter, but it is all lies. The winter cold is a different cold, and there is nothing brisk or refreshing about the wind blowing off the water. The moisture that makes the summer so miserable makes the winters unlivable. They talk about the old houses, the fine sturdy construction, but they never say that the old gray bricks hold the moisture until it seeps into every pore, sending the damp cold into every corner of every room. The only warmth you find is from a small gas space heater that makes eyes burn and sends out noxious fumes, choking lungs, strangling the throat. But then Savannah sends one of her daughters, and you cannot leave when you are huddled under the covers with such a pretty face, telling you to stay until spring.

Once spring comes, Savannah is totally in charge. It is in the spring that she remembers her youth, and even the dusty old slums and unpaved streets come alive. For it is her flowers, the azaleas, that are massive, erupting in the parks and beside every street. Savannah is no proper Southern lady. She is no prim delicate thing, planting her peonies in the yard, hoping for a few spring blossoms. Her true personality comes out, and she is loud and overbearing. These are no subtle womanly charms that she possesses. Her colors are bold, demanding, mirroring her personality. She has no need of her daughters in springtime. She can hold her own with any competition.

But Savannah is at her best in the fall. She does not try to exhaust with the heat, does not try to whip into submission with her cold, northeast winds, does not try to dull the senses with her shocking hues. In the fall, she is herself. The beach is not crowded, the weather is pleasing, and her daughters are their prettiest. Everyone is alive, not beaten down by her whims. It would be difficult to leave her in the fall. But winter is coming. It is time for you to leave. Savannah has kept too many of her young men until they cannot leave. You must go, for there is a chance and you cannot pass it by.

5

Durham

Durham was ready. For years, it has been the blue-collar vertex of the Raleigh-Durham-Chapel Hill "Triangle." Raleigh was the state capital with government jobs and North Carolina State University. Chapel Hill had the University of North Carolina and prided itself on being the "Southern part of heaven." Durham had American Tobacco and Liggett & Myers tobacco factories along with textile mills and minimum-wage workers. Duke University was part of Durham, but barely. It isolated itself on the western edge of the city and rarely interacted with the town. By 1980, folks were turning away from Chesterfield and Lucky Strikes, and the two huge tobacco factories in downtown Durham, which had at one point been running three shifts a day, had barely enough business for one shift. The cavernous tobacco auction warehouses near the ballpark were mostly shuttered, and almost all of the textile business had moved to Mexico.

The city could have become like many northeastern Rust Belt cities, dying but hanging on with little hope for the future. But there was energy in Durham. Citizens knew that Raleigh and Chapel Hill turned up their noses at their poor relation, but civic leaders believed Durham had something special. The mix of people was real. A Black entrepreneurial tradition, fostered by North Carolina Central University, had been part of the city for decades. Now, Duke graduates were not leaving the city after graduation but staying and starting businesses. The sons and daughters of tobacco workers were also staying in the city and looking for better opportunities. City government was progressive and encouraged new business in the community.

Durham needed a spark to ignite this energy. By 2020, Durham was recognized as one of the top mid-sized cities in the United States. No one element or incident caused this growth from a dying tobacco town to a major city. A combination of efforts and individuals helped the city transform itself. But many would argue that the Durham Bulls were the first spark that set off this growth. It was not instantaneous, and in the

There's a Bulldozer on Home Plate

first few years, the flames that the Bulls were building could have died, but the success of the franchise spurred other business. By the end of the decade, the Bulls were a national phenomenon, helping to push a city that was markedly changing and growing.

Arriving in Durham in the fall of 1979, I had no visions of what Durham could become. My goal was simply to survive. With ten years of experience in the business, I knew what I could do as an operator. With a city the size of Durham, then 100,000, I believed the team could average around 1,000 fans a game which would be enough to break even. I now had the franchise, the working agreement with the Atlanta Braves, and a lease with the city on the ballpark. The one thing I didn't have was money.

Business schools teach that to start a small business, an entrepreneur needs to have sufficient capital before signing leases and making agreements. Fortunately, no one asked to see financial statements. I did have enough to pay the league $2,417, the price of the franchise. No further investigation was done on my financial background. At this point, the league was just happy to have a warm body to take over the club. The conventional wisdom within the Carolina League was that I was buying the right to lose money and league directors silently hoped the franchise could make it to the end of the season.

I did understand that enough money was needed to get to Opening Day, and I started efforts to raise capital. At first, my efforts were directed to finding local investors. Local ownership can be important in the success of a club, but Durham businessmen had owned prior teams, and no one in the city seemed willing to invest in another minor league venture. It was then that I started approaching family and friends. Two friends and former minor league owners, Van Schley and Joe Helyar, each put in $5,000. Van suggested that a friend of his on the West Coast, Thom Mount, might be interested. Thom was a producer for Universal Pictures and a Durham native. I made contact, and Thom also was willing to put in $5,000. Three of my buddies from growing up in Greensboro each put in $1,000 as did my father and two sisters. To gain further funds, I sold much of the stock my mother had left me, and by the end of these efforts, I had a little over $30,000 to set up and run the Durham Bulls baseball club. That should be enough to start the business. Optimism is always great to have.

I had never owned a business before and knew nothing about corporations. I was a history major, which was not coming in handy. I needed a legal entity to operate within. With no lawyer, Thom Mount, the new

5. Durham

investor, suggested I go see his father, who was an attorney. Checking around town, I found that Lillard Mount was one of the leading lawyers in Durham. I knew that I would not be able to afford him, but Thom kept insisting I go meet with him. I made an appointment and went to see Mr. Mount. He was in his sixties—graying, pipe-smoking, and thoughtful—and he listened as I told him what I planned to do with the Bulls. He asked if I wanted a C Corp, a Sub-S corporation, or partnership. I paused and told him I needed to think about it. Another meeting was arranged.

I quickly found a bookstore and purchased a Cliffs Notes on business. I had no idea what Mr. Mount was talking about, and it was clear I needed some basic knowledge. Returning for the next meeting, I was a bit more informed, and the relationship with Mr. Mount became one of the most valuable contacts I would have in the coming years. His advice on legal and other subjects helped in so many ways, and he truly was a counselor. In later years when I had to deal with various lawyers, none were the equal of Mr. Mount.

I had been worried about the legal fees, and Mr. Mount proposed an annual retainer of $600 a year. That seemed reasonable, and he became the team lawyer. Later I would find out that his yearly retainer for the Bulls was nearly the same as some attorneys' hourly fee. Over the years, I would spend many hours with Mr. Mount, but the retainer never changed.

The ballpark offices in Durham were two small plywood rooms at the top of the grandstand that overlooked the field. I took one of the offices and named myself president. The other needed to be filled with a general manager. Jim Mills, president of the league, suggested one of his umpires might be a good choice for that position: Pete Bock, a Durham native. For the previous three seasons he had been a minor league umpire and a good one. But Pete was married with a young son, and the climb to the big leagues was a particularly long, tough road for umpires. He wanted to stay in the game, and the Durham front office job would be a good opportunity for him. Umpires in the minor leagues know the score, and several had made the switch to the minor league front office with success. I interviewed Pete and decided to take him on as GM. It was a good hire.

Over the fall Pete and I began work on sales and promotions, and the response was encouraging. Durham seemed to want the team. I had always liked cities that had a baseball history with fathers passing on their love of the team to their sons and daughters. Fans started stopping by the office to buy tickets and some commented that their fathers brought them to Bulls games when they were young. Now these fans would be able to bring their children and experience the same joy they had found at the ballpark. It was a good feeling.

That winter, Thom Mount came to Durham to visit his parents and stopped by the ballpark to view his investment. Thom was very personable, and he was excited about the potential of the Bulls. As a young boy, he attended many games. He proposed that one of the costume designers at Universal Pictures, Marilyn Vance, could design the uniforms and suggested that artists at MCA records might be able to design the logo. We had made no headway on uniforms or logo, and our answer was a quick yes. Then, in a thoughtful mood, he proposed an idea that I had never considered. "Miles, someday we should make a movie here. Wouldn't that be good." I nodded yes but silently wondered if this wasn't just Hollywood talking. Movies aren't made in minor league ballparks.

Positive developments kept happening. The Atlanta Braves announced that Al Gallagher was to be the Bulls' manager. This was important. "Dirty Al" was colorful and believed in winning. Many minor league managers were the opposite. The morning newspaper assigned a young sportswriter, Ron Morris, to the beat. He began writing articles on the history of the team, giving us extra exposure in the preseason. He was sent to spring training in Florida and two stories a day were published on the Bulls' training camp.

In another piece of good fortune, a publisher accepted my novel, *Season of the Owl*. It would be published in the spring. It was a coming-of-age story of a young boy in North Carolina and a minor league club hit by racial protests. The book ultimately went through four editions, including one in Japanese. If the acceptance had come six months earlier, I might have stayed at the beach to continue writing. However, any thoughts of writing were pushed to the back. The Bulls consumed all my time and I was recapturing the joy of running a baseball team.

The operation clicked into gear and was running smoothly. Everything was positive except in one area. We ran out of money in March. We were selling well, but sponsors were waiting until Opening Day to pay. The city's contract stated that the rent must be paid up front. They weren't dummies. Costs for concessions equipment and other items were more than was budgeted, and I found myself waking up at 4 a.m. most mornings, unable to go back to sleep, wondering if the operation could make it to April and Opening Day. I approached Pete Bock to let him know the situation.

5. Durham

"Pete, I've got good news and bad news for you. Which do you want to hear first?"

"Let's hear the good news first."

"You've been doing a really good job. I am raising your salary to $900 a month." He had been making $700.

"Ok. Great. Thank you. Now what's the bad news?"

You hesitate. "Pete, we are out of money. I won't be able to pay you until after the opener. Can you make it until then?"

He grimaced. "Sure. We'll make it."

Then it was necessary to inform the league president and let him know the situation. We were behind in league dues and unable to pay. Rather than become upset, he quietly checked the league treasury and without consulting other league directors, lent the operation $4,000. It was a godsend. I could now possibly make it to Opening Day. Once the games began, it would simply be a matter of drawing enough people to see if the Bulls survived.

Everything began piling up as Opening Day approached. We needed employees, but with little money, students at nearby colleges who would accept minimum wage became the staff. One Duke undergrad became the concessions manager, another the business manager, and a former Carolina student, Bill Miller, would become the longtime groundskeeper for the Bulls. None had any experience in their respective jobs, but their eagerness trumped lack of experience. The play-by-play announcer's wife became the secretary and receptionist. My office was moved to the top of the tower ("donjon," as one writer described it) in front of the stadium. In need of storage, we rented an old store across the street which also became the souvenir store, "Ballpark Corner." With cash non-existent, we traded out with a local dairy for an old milk truck. The dairy received a fence sign. By drilling holes in the side of the truck and attaching beer taps to the front, this became our main beer stand. With the compressor the only part that worked on the truck, our beer kegs were kept cold, and the milk truck saw service for thirty years.

Two days before the opener, disaster reared its head. The health inspector arrived and announced that we would not be able to open concessions unless we had an ice machine. Our plan had been to buy bagged ice from a local distributor. Now, without ice we would not be able to sell soft drinks and without soft drinks, we would have no concessions and without concessions, we would be out of business. Buying a $2,000 ice-making machine was simply out of the question. Pete

There's a Bulldozer on Home Plate

saw me sitting in the grandstand with my head in my hands and knew things were not right. The health inspector was still on-site, and Pete rushed up to him. I never found out what was said, but when the inspector departed, the bagged ice was allowed.

We had just received the uniforms from Hollywood, and as Thom Mount described them, they were "hot." Made from Spandex, they appeared to glow in the dark. Three nights before Opening Day, the team had an open workout under the lights, and the uniforms looked great. Unfortunately, in the middle of that night, someone broke into our clubhouse and stole all the home uniforms and some of the players' equipment. The world was crashing in. I called Hank Aaron, the Braves farm director, and he found an old set of Braves uniforms that he rushed up to Durham. The thieves had not stolen our new set of shiny dark blue road uniforms, and we were able to wear these for the home games. On the road, we became the Durham Braves. I had no insurance for the uniforms. I placed a call to Marilyn Vance, who had designed the uniforms, and she let me know she could have a new set in six weeks. I hoped she would wait until then to bill the club.

The other major catastrophe was the grass. When I first toured the ballpark nine months earlier, little grass was visible on the infield. The city agreed to re-sod the infield. In the fall, the city re-sodded with Bermuda, which is a fine grass. Regrettably, Bermuda does not turn green until the warm summer months, and in April the Durham Athletic Park infield looked like a brown checkerboard. We definitely needed green grass for the opener. Someone suggested that the infield could be spray-painted green, and spectators would not know the difference. With no knowledge to back up this suggestion, a spray paint machine was rented. The paint worked, although now there was a green checkerboard infield. The only negative was the fact that the paint did not dry quickly and baseballs that bounced through the infield resembled large, lime-green Easter eggs.

Opening Night, a Tuesday, was cold—45 degrees at game time. The usual pre-game festivities with bands and speakers were held, and the ceremonies only lasted 10 minutes past schedule. I had no feel for the potential crowd, but the fans kept streaming in, and the stadium with a listed capacity of 5,000 looked full. We announced 4,410, and the money was outstanding.

Murphy's Law is written for minor league openers, and disasters were part of the Opening Night experience. In the sixth inning, the toilets stopped working. Apparently, the city had installed the wrong-sized

5. Durham

water line into the ballpark, and the toilets could not keep up with the crowd. In the seventh inning the field lights cut out, and the field was bathed in darkness. The wrong circuit breaker had been installed. A city electrician was on-site, and his short-term solution was to stick his screwdriver in the breaker to keep the connection open. The breaker box was attached to the side of the grandstand and fans, unaware, were walking beside the electrician as he held his screwdriver in the live box until the game ended. It was not a solution that would normally have been approved by those who have to approve that sort of thing. But it worked.

The first night was a win and the atmosphere was great. The second night, we drew 642, and on Thursday, the crowd was 884, but I was not disappointed. Both were good money crowds, and with the temperature in the low 40s, it was encouraging. On Friday the draw was 2,316, much more than expected, and the crowd seemed exceptionally lively. The beer seemed to help. These were enthusiastic fans, and a group of Duke law school students started the chant "Let's go Bulls!" Other fans began picking up on the cheer.

By Saturday, something had clicked in the community. At 7:00 Pete Bock and I were out in the parking lot where the line to buy tickets was literally a city block long. The ballpark was full for the 7:30 game and every seat was taken. Pete announced that most seating was gone with only standing room and berm seating left. No one left the line. The crowd wanted to come in. If fans didn't care about seats, we certainly were ready to sell them tickets. The stadium had a grassy berm behind the left field wall and fans sat on the ground and watched the game from there. No one complained.

The promotion that night was Jacket Night, with every child 14 and under getting a free, cheap vinyl jacket. We had ordered 1,000 jackets and they were gone. Normally, a giveaway might attract 500 to 1,000 in extra attendance, but something was special about this crowd. People were at the game to see baseball. My experience in the past with giveaway nights was that the crowd was primarily attending the game for the free stuff. The fans would basically sit on their hands, waiting for the seventh inning so they could have an excuse to leave. These fans in Durham were staying, having a great time, and taking up the chant "Let's Go Bulls" in unison. It almost felt like the big leagues. We announced 5,791 in attendance with every space in the grandstand, bleachers, and behind the outfield wall taken.

The first month was spectacular. We were successful beyond my

There's a Bulldozer on Home Plate

"Dirty Al" Gallagher, the colorful manager of the resurrected Durham Bulls for the 1980 and 1981 seasons.

wildest hopes. The team was in first place and at one point won 12 straight games. "Dirty Al" Gallagher had the team stealing bases at every opportunity, and the speed was intimidating other teams. The crowds were happy and into the games. An important reason was beer. This was the first time it had ever been legal to sell beer at a baseball game in Durham. North Carolina was fairly regressive when it came to liquor laws, and the city of Durham had passed liquor by the drink only a few years earlier. A few bars were opening up in the city, and one newspaper headlined Durham Athletic Park as "The Best Bar in Town."

I also learned something about Pete Bock that sounded like it was out of The *Twilight Zone*. His grandfather was buried on the pitching mound. It was true. His grandfather, a minor league pitcher named Claude "Buck" Weaver, won 18 games for Durham in 1946. He started in the minors in 1928 and was a professional pitcher until he was almost 50. When he died in 1967, his body was cremated and his ashes were raked into the mound at Durham Athletic Park. Now his

5. Durham

grandson was the general manager at his grandfather's burial site. Strange. (Even stranger, 15 years later the pitcher in the final Carolina League game ever played at the DAP was Jeff Bock, then a prospect for the Atlanta Braves. Jeff was Pete's son and the great-grandson of Buck Weaver.)

The first season ended as well as it started. Everything seemed to go our way. The team finished in first place in its division for both halves of the season and made the playoffs. With no funds, we had no field tarp that season, yet there were only two rainouts. Both were on Monday nights in April when the crowds were normally sparse. In the following years, the club bought a full infield tarp and even with that protection, six or seven rainouts occurred each season. Both morning and evening newspapers sent writers to cover the team daily and the Bulls were always one of the leading sports stories. Manager "Dirty Al" Gallagher, always colorful, was the poster child for the team.

For seven years after I left the Savannah Braves, I bounced from club to club with little success. Then the Durham Bulls came, and luck seemed to turn. I was on a wave, and I was going to ride it as far as it would take me. Each year the Bulls' attendance increased, and it provided the funds to pursue other ventures. Although several clubs such as Columbus, Ohio, and Nashville, Tennessee, were remarkable success stories, minor league baseball was still not recognized as a place to make money. The rich guys had not yet invaded the sport. Clubs were available, ready to pick up on the cheap, and the Bulls became the vehicle to expand into other areas of minor league baseball.

In 1981 the Bulls bought majority control of the Asheville Tourists of the South Atlantic League for $10,000 and in 1982 picked up the Utica Blue Sox of the New York–Pennsylvania League for debts. The Atlanta Braves needed a rookie league team in the Appalachian League, and we started a team in little Pulaski, Virginia, with no investment. A minor league baseball newspaper, the *All-America Baseball News,* was struggling and the Bulls entered the publishing business for debts and a visa. We renamed the paper *Baseball America,* and it grew. In the next few years, we also bought the Butte (Montana) Copper Kings of the Pioneer League and were close to acquiring a Double-A Eastern League franchise with a timed payment plan until the owner became nervous and wanted his money up front. The goal with all these clubs was to put them on a good business foundation, and when they were profitable, sell them. It was before the huge spike in franchise values, and the organization ended up making a modest profit on all the clubs.

There's a Bulldozer on Home Plate

One club that we acquired but needed patience was in Burlington, North Carolina. When the woebegone Rocky Mount Pines folded after going 24–114 during the 1980 season, the Carolina League was desperate to find a city to replace that team. The league president searched throughout North Carolina and Virginia trying to find a stadium, but no city would accept the team. He asked for help from league members, and I decided to look at Burlington as an option. The old ballpark was still standing, but I knew no one in the city. I did know Jack McKeon, then the GM of the San Diego Padres, who made his permanent residence in Burlington. I called Jack and he gave me the number of a city council member who would soon become mayor.

Never had I met a political leader with so much enthusiasm for bringing baseball to his city. Unfortunately, it was January and Fairchild Park was in such bad shape that there was no way to get it ready for an April opening, nor had any funds been allocated. In the meantime, the Carolina League president had found a replacement city: Hagerstown, Maryland. But with a mayor so enthusiastic, I could not stop my efforts, and I started work on bringing baseball to the city.

With confidence that a team would become available, I worked out a lease and was paying the rent on the lease. Obtaining the lease was a problem because we needed to be able to sell beer in the stadium. Beer had never been available in prior years. Opposition arose, and at the city council meeting where the motion to approve the lease was to be considered, forty Baptist ministers showed up in opposition. The mayor was a good Baptist, and he thought he had the votes to pass the lease without needing to vote himself. However, one councilman, in favor of baseball but opposed to the mayor, changed his vote and the motion came down to the mayor's vote. The mayor was squirming as he looked at the forty reverends on one side and me on the other. Finally, he voted yes, certain he was damned to perdition. The lease was approved.

Over the next three years we worked diligently to bring baseball to Burlington. The Braves were close to moving their Sally League team to the city, but it was blocked by Greensboro ownership. The Carolina League had several clubs ready to move but all fell through. By 1985 I was ready to give up but heard that a club in the Rookie-level Appalachian League might be available. The Appalachian League had always hosted cities in the mountains of Virginia, West Virginia, and Tennessee, and Burlington was viewed by league directors as being outside of its footprint. The Cleveland Indians were ready to put a team in one of the league's traditional cities but stepped back when the mayor of that city

5. Durham

informed the farm director that the city would be unable to provide housing for Black players. I placed a call to the farm director who, blindsided by a viewpoint he believed had died decades earlier, was desperate to find a city. We quickly reached agreement and Burlington had pro baseball. For the next thirty-five years, I would be owner and president of the team.

Each city was different, but we tried to put in a good front office staff and hopefully turn the operations around. It was not always easy. We took over the Utica Blue Sox to help Van Schley who was supplying independent players to Utica. No major league club wanted to send players to Murnane Field, the city's inadequate ballpark. The sun set in the first baseman's eyes, the right-field foul pole was only 260 feet from home plate, and dressing rooms were deep beyond the right-field fence. We also needed funds to pay the prior year's debts. The word floating around baseball was that Roger Kahn, the author of *The Boys of Summer*, the terrific read on the Brooklyn Dodgers, had been given an advance by a publisher to write a book on minor league baseball. The premise for the book was that Roger would be the Walter O'Malley, the Dodgers' owner, of the minor leagues, but he needed a minor league club to name him general manager.

No affiliated club was willing to have an untested, best-selling author run their operations. The Utica club was not proud and offered him the position of GM if he would pay the prior year's electric bill of nearly $10,000. We needed lights to be able to start the season and he needed a team to get his advance. Kahn became GM. His abilities in that role were limited and he occasionally needed help in decision-making, with aid coming from a bottle in his desk drawer. However, a book came out of that season, *Good Enough to Dream*. The title came from the assistant GM's response to Kahn's question, "How good are your players?" The Blue Sox survived the year and were sold.

Everything seemed to be falling my way. Then something non-baseball entered the picture. In 1981, I met Michelle Guimond. After a game I was visiting a bar and restaurant which owed the team for its advertising. The owner had bought a fence sign but now was behind in paying. I was sitting at the bar with a beer, politely reminding him of the need to pay, while he avoided the subject and introduced me to a girl also sitting at the bar. She was one of the waitresses who had finished her shift for the evening and was having a drink. We chatted for a while, and she invited me to a birthday party for a co-worker that was being held later that evening. I went, enjoyed the late evening, and didn't think much more about it. A few days later, she came to a game with a girlfriend. We chatted briefly, but during a game I was totally occupied, and could spend little time with her. She asked if she could bring some of her clients to a future game. My answer was yes, not certain what "clients" she was talking about.

Michelle's full-time job was at the Murdoch Center in Butner, North Carolina, where she was a teacher in a section of the state institution that handled the severely challenged. She worked with blind and deaf kids, those who were self-injurious, and all of whom had special needs. These were her "clients." She began bringing these children to the games and it was amazing to see the joy on their faces as they entered this strange world of a minor league stadium. They were coming from an antiseptic institutional environment with little sensory stimulation. At the ballpark the unexpected smell of hot dogs and popcorn and beer wafted through the concourse. The sounds of a crowd yelling and the music from the PA were not part of their everyday life, and it was almost always delight that registered on their faces. The stadium lights were fascinating and even the visually impaired kids could see some of the streams of light in their darkness.

One kid, Jimmy, was particularly memorable. He was blind and did not communicate well, but one evening he spread his joy to everyone nearby. The concession stands used paper cups to serve soft drinks. Some fans would occasionally stomp on these cups to make a loud popping noise. That night, a young fan popped a paper cup near Jimmy. He was startled but then let out a huge laugh. It was infectious. Another kid, hearing the laugh, brought another cup nearby and also popped it. Again, Jimmy laughed his special laugh and by game's end, kids from all over the stadium were bringing cups just to hear Jimmy laugh. It remains one of my all-time favorite games.

I previously had little contact with this population and was certainly not comfortable dealing with special needs kids. Yet, Michelle acted as if it is the most natural thing in the world. She hugged these kids, talked to them, and sometimes just the touch of her hand on the arm was enough to calm them, to let them know she was near. She understood their needs. I was amazed.

One game she came by herself, and because she was alone, I had her sit with Lillard and Bonnie Mount. I would come and sit for a half inning or so, but she and the Mounts were comfortable together and they liked her. That mattered. For the next year the dating continued, and I found myself really liking this girl. It was time to do what I had to do. I broke up with Michelle.

5. Durham

Getting married had never been on my bucket list, and Michelle and I were getting too close. Baseball and a wife did not mix in my book, and in the past when a girl was getting serious, it was always time to move to the next team. But the Bulls were going great, and I knew I would be in Durham for more than three years. A girl would tie me down. Michelle had difficulty understanding my reasoning.

A few weeks after breaking up, I returned to the restaurant where she was still working part-time. I had not expected to see her and was uncertain how she would react. She was friendly as always. More importantly, I was surprised at how glad I was to see her. It was all over. We were married the following February. The reception was held at the restaurant where the owner still had not paid for the fence sign. He catered the reception, did not charge, and more than paid back what was owed.

The next year, my son, Hoffman, was born, and the following year my daughter, Claire. From infancy, Michelle brought them to almost every game. Hoffman was keeping score by age five while Claire would play with her dolls or color while the game progressed. Claire would tolerate the baseball-centric life, but there were times when it was a bit too much. We were driving to Maine one summer to visit Michelle's family, and along the way I had scheduled a few baseball stops. An all-star game in Frederick, Maryland; a meeting with the GM in Scranton, Pennsylvania; and a chance to see a game in Oneonta, New York, were all part of the plan. Cooperstown was too close not to visit, and we made a detour to the Baseball Hall of Fame. It was too much for Claire. At age 6, she was at her breaking point. In the middle of displays of baseball immortals, this little girl stopped and announced to all present, "I hate baseball! I hate baseball!" In this sacred shrine, the blasphemy was too much and with glares from other patrons, we quickly shuffled to an exit.

The fun of running any business is to see it succeed, but with a minor league club, involvement in the community is important and ownership becomes a great way to know the city and the people. I only owned Asheville for two seasons and then sold it for $75,000, but the memories of a beautiful mountain city with a rickety old wooden ballpark are strong. A husband-and-wife team ran the club and did an excellent job in keeping the baseball in the city. It was in Asheville where I met an old major league player, Shag Thompson, who had long-ago ties to the Durham Bulls.

There's a Bulldozer on Home Plate

Bulls Illustrated (June/July 1982)
"Shag Thompson"

You are in Asheville for the Opening Day of the Asheville Tourists when an old man approaches. He has heard you are with the Durham Bulls, and he is carrying something in a brown grocery bag. He reaches in and pulls out an old photograph in a plain, black frame. He hands it to you, and it is a picture of a baseball team, the 1913 Durham Bulls, standing before a huge wooden billboard for Bull Durham smoking tobacco. There are thirteen team members, each with arms hanging at their sides. He points to one of the figures, third from the left, a short, chunky individual, young and pleasant-faced. It is the old man, 70 years earlier.

At first, it is the picture that captures your interest, for you have never seen one of the legendary "Bull Durham" billboards. It is where the nickname "bullpen" derived and you sit with the old man to study the ancient billboard. It is the only fence sign in an old ballpark in West Durham, and the board is monstrous, over 20 feet high, a fully equipped bull that towers over the team in front. The old man starts talking, as old men often do, and your attention shifts.

His name is James Thompson, but that is not a name for a ballplayer, and for most of his life he has been known as "Shag." He is now 89. He talks of his years in baseball, a young player signed out of the University of North Carolina by Judge William Bramham to play for the Durham Bulls. A year later he is with the Philadelphia Athletics, a team that will win the American League pennant. He is alert and clear-eyed, a man whom the years have been kind to. As he talks, as he sits and remembers, the years slip away, and he is once again breaking into the American League.

It is difficult to describe the sensation as you listen, for it is as if you have been placed in a time machine, and the occasional chill is not from the cool spring evening. He is talking of Connie Mack and Ty Cobb and Walter Johnson as if it had only been last week when he was on the diamond with them. He is a link to a baseball past you had only read about, an era you have never had any contact with.

But for Shag Thompson, that time is very much alive, and as with many old ballplayers, he can remember the pitch, the weather, everything associated with those important games. He talks of the 1914 World Series as the Athletics lost four straight to the Boston "Miracle" Braves, and as he shakes his head, the defeat is still there. He is once more taking the long train ride back to Philly after the losses in Boston, the whole team drinking their sorrows away. Chief Bender, Frank "Home Run" Baker and Eddie Collins were all on that team, but Shag Thompson is the only member still alive.

Connie Mack first played in the major leagues in 1886 and died over a quarter of a century ago, but for Thompson, the memories and antipathy

5. *Durham*

are strong. Connie Mack brought him to the big leagues, was his first major league manager, but Thompson's contract battles with Mack may be the reason why his major league career lasted only parts of the 1914, 1915, and 1916 seasons. With the Federal league forming in late 1914, Thompson signed a $5,000 contract with the Athletics out of loyalty to Mack, rather than jump to the St. Louis club of the Federal League for $7,500. But when the Federals folded, Mack tried to renegotiate Thompson's contract to $200 a week. Thompson fought it hard, and Mack then shipped him to Omaha. Later, Roger Bresnahan of the Chicago Cubs tried to get Thompson's contract, but Mack blocked the deal. Again, you forget the time factor, this long-ago era seeming like yesterday until it hits you that the Roger Bresnahan he is talking about is the catcher who invented shin guards.

The stories roll out. He recounts Ty Cobb congratulating him when, as a rookie, he threw out Cobb at second base from deep right field. He remembers fouling fourteen straight pitches off Walter Johnson until the "Big Train" struck him out. And he remembers Jack Dunn.

Jack Dunn was one of the great minor league managers, winning pennants for seven straight seasons for the old Baltimore Orioles of the International League. But Shag Thompson does not remember Jack Dunn kindly. He still blames the old Oriole manager for his brief major league career. In 1915 Connie Mack farmed Thompson out to Dunn's club, playing that season in Richmond because the Federal League had invaded Baltimore. It was a team of old veterans that finished seventh, and Thompson was in the manager's doghouse much of the season. On one occasion, he and Chick Fewster missed a ferry boat to the Toronto ballpark and were late arriving for batting practice. But Thompson's eyes glow as he remembers how he showed up Dunn. In the seventh inning of that game, benched because of the missed ferry, Thompson was called off the bench by Dunn to pinch hit. The old man still sees his triple off the right center field wall, knocking in the winning run.

Thompson now lives in Black Mountain, N.C., and he has been driven over to Asheville that night to throw out the opening pitch for the first game of the season. You borrow the picture to have a copy made and make arrangements to return it to him the next day. When you arrive at his home, he has his scrapbook ready. He started it when he was in high school, and he has pictures of himself on the Trinity College team. He did not like Trinity (now Duke University) and transferred to the University of North Carolina. The scrapbook is well-worn, and he talks about the entries as he turns the pages. The major league career was over after 1916, but he played professionally until 1923, and the clippings headline "Shag Thompson" leading the Western League and the Three-I League in hitting. There are the minor league towns, and he played in Omaha, Columbus, Nashville, Moline, Bloomington, and more until he retired.

After leaving baseball he settled in Asheville, and with half a dozen

There's a Bulldozer on Home Plate

Durham Bulls, 1913. This is the team photograph of the 1913 Bulls that was given by James "Shag" Thompson to Miles Wolff in 1982. Thompson is the player third from the right. Future major leaguer pitcher Lee "Spec" Meadows is sixth from right.

different jobs in the years through the Depression and World War II, he was successful and now leads a comfortable retirement. He married a girl from Haw River early in his baseball career, and she traveled with him to all the minor league stops. When she died a few years ago, he was alone. He has now remarried, and his new wife enjoys his pursuits of fishing and gardening. The front lawn is full of flowers, and the house is immaculate.

As with many older men who have kept their faculties, who remain alert, you can sense a tinge of frustration. He has so much to tell, has learned so much over the years, and now there are very few to listen, no one to learn. So he contents himself with his flowers and his fishing and an occasional look at an old scrapbook.

As you get up to go to your car, he walks with you and talks about "the love of the game." It is just baseball he is talking about, but it is still a part of him after all these years. It is the common bond, the link that stretches from Connie Mack who caught his first minor league game around 1880 to the 19-year-old catcher on the Asheville Tourists who caught Thompson's toss of the ceremonial first pitch in 1982. It is a bond that tied the 1913 Bulls to the 1982 club. It is a bond that ties you to a baseball past. You leave and begin the drive back to Durham.

5. Durham

The Bulls continued to grow. Our corporation was running other ballclubs, but the Bulls were the bread and butter. Attendance kept increasing as concessions and restroom space were added. Parking never increased but our fans did not seem to care. It was part of the ambiance, finding a parking space in a nearby lot or street. The Carolina League always scheduled 70 home dates, but we worked to bring other baseball events to the park. Wrestling and boxing were tried, but baseball was the best attraction. Team USA was becoming one of the leaders in baseball for quality collegiate players, and that organization needed venues to play international teams. When no one else would give guarantees, the Bulls did and teams with such future stars as Will Clark and Jose Canseco played at the DAP. International teams from Japan and Korea came, and Durham Athletic Park was one of the first venues in the United States to host Cuba's national team.

The Atlantic Coast Conference baseball tournament was a moneyloser for the conference, traditionally being held at the UNC campus where many teams could commute, enabling the ACC to save money. It was an opportunity for us, and I met with the coaches and promised to pay all expenses plus $10,000 if the conference would move the tournament to Durham. The offer was met with more than mild skepticism, but the coaches were willing to give it a try. The tournament at Durham Athletic Park proved a huge success in the neutral site. Seeing the success, minor league venues all over the Southeast bid on the tournament the following year. With these larger facilities, the Bulls were effectively priced out of holding the competition. It was disappointing, but there was some satisfaction. We believed baseball was a great spectator sport with the right promotion and incentives and proved it with the ACC tournament, Team USA, international contests, and the Bulls.

The Bulls were riding high. Everything seemed to be bouncing our way. It was difficult to think that the organization could do much better. Then the movie came to Durham.

6

The Movie

In the fall of 1979 when Thom Mount invested in the Durham Bulls and made the comment, "Someday we will make a movie here," I silently dismissed the statement as just Hollywood talking. The movie industry wasn't making baseball movies and certainly not in Durham, North Carolina. Then in the summer of 1986, Thom called and let me know that he was sending a screenwriter to Durham to get a taste of minor league baseball. No indication was given that plans were in the works for a movie in Durham. Thom simply had a baseball script on his desk that needed more minor league flavor.

The screenwriter was Ron Shelton, a former player in the Baltimore Orioles organization. He was good enough to have reached Triple-A, but the call to the big leagues never came. He changed professions and ultimately became a screenwriter. Ron certainly knew the minor leagues, but the two weeks he spent with the Bulls brought him back to his first passion. He sat on the bench for most games, and at times would take batting practice. He was in his element. He wandered around Durham, and by the end of his trip, he was convinced his script should be made in the city. He appreciated the grittiness of the old tobacco factories and a ballpark that was pure minor league. He adjusted his script. It did not take much convincing to have Thom Mount agree that the picture should be made in Durham. Ron was named director of the picture although he had never directed a film before.

The studio producing the film, Orion, was not particularly high on the project. Orion had another baseball film in production, *Eight Men Out*, and had high hopes for that film. Thom Mount became the producer for the Shelton film and the studio gave him an $8 million budget, not particularly generous for a full-length feature film. The leads in the film were Kevin Costner, Susan Sarandon, and Tim Robbins, fringe stars at the time. Durham Athletic Park became the main setting for the film, and the Bulls received a minor location fee of $10,000. The Bulls' staff called other minor league parks in the area, and these sites and the

6. The Movie

uniforms of their teams were used in the film at no cost. Pete Bock, who had been the first GM of the Bulls, was back in Durham working on new projects for the Bulls organization, and he became the baseball consultant for the film.

Filming started in September, after the Bulls' season had finished, and the front office staff was dedicated to helping the movie people. Many of the players stuck around to be part of the different baseball teams in the filming, and the grounds crew set up and put the field in condition for the different scenes. Pete Bock actually had to fill in as a member of the cast. On one evening shoot, a wedding scene, it was discovered that an actor had not been hired to play the minister. The costume for the scene was ready, and because Pete was the only one around who fit the minister's suit, he became an actor, pronouncing the couple "man and wife." He quickly joined the Screen Actors Guild and for years afterwards he would receive a modest royalty check.

In the first draft of the screenplay, Shelton had written a scene that called for a character that mirrored Max Patkin, a longtime baseball comedy act who had been touring the minor leagues since the late 1940s. I had read the screenplay and suggested to Ron that he hire the original "Clown Prince of Baseball." Ron had seen Max's act many times when he was playing minor league ball but did not realize Max was still alive. Ron was elated at the possibility. I called Max, and he was eager to be part of the movie. His career lasted another five years from the publicity he gained from the movie.

The working title on the script was *Bull Durham*. Another title was expected to be given the movie but as production moved along, the name just seemed to fit and was retained.

Normally, fall is the best season for weather in North Carolina. The temperatures are mild, and rain is not a problem. The fall of 1987, however, was one of the coldest in memory, and actors' breaths were visible in many of the night scenes. Tim Robbins was wearing only a jockstrap in a scene on one of the coldest nights of that fall. It was not a comfortable evening for the actor. The trees turned early that year, and for a summer sport, it was a little jarring to see yellow and red trees in the background.

Working with the movie people was not always easy. Several times, trucks from the production wanted to take equipment onto the infield. Grounds personnel for the Bulls had to confront the drivers and push them back to keep the vehicles from destroying the turf that needed to be protected for the following season. One scene called for a large crowd in the stands, and Bulls staff sent out letters to season ticket holders and fans to encourage them to come and be part of the shoot. A free hot dog was promised. When a crowd of nearly 2,000 assembled on a Saturday afternoon, someone in the production crew decided it should be a night scene. The staff was told not to give out hot dogs until six hours later in hopes that the crowd would stay. This was not going to happen. The announcement was made that the shooting was delayed, hot dogs were available, and the hope was that most fans would stick around. The crowd for the night scene was not large.

The production took almost two months, and at the end, I was ready for the movie folks to leave. I personally was not certain *Bull Durham* would ever be released. It was frustrating to see the movie folks work, and last-minute changes and confusion during the shooting made one wonder if the crew knew what they were doing. At the start of the filming, it was exciting to be around, but by the end I avoided the set and stayed in my office at *Baseball America* rather than the ballpark. Thom Mount was in California for most of the shooting, but he assured me that everything was going well. I had my doubts.

The following spring, *Bull Durham* was set for release with the grand premiere being held in Durham at the venerable Carolina Theatre downtown. I rented a tuxedo and Michelle bought a new dress. In the theater we sat with Lillard and Bonnie Mount, Thom Mount's parents. I was nervous. With misgivings about the produc-

Ticket for the June 15, 1988, premiere of *Bull Durham* at the Carolina Theatre.

6. The Movie

tion at the ballpark, I wondered if the movie was going to be a flop. Would it be embarrassing? Michelle was sitting next to Mrs. Mount, a very sweet and proper Southern lady. In an early scene, Nuke and Millie sneak off to the clubhouse for a bit of non-baseball activity. Michelle could sense Mrs. Mount tensing. Was this going to be the movie's theme? I relaxed slightly as the film continued, and at the end, Michelle and I thought it probably had been OK. But we certainly weren't positive. A week later, we decided to go see the movie again and try to get a non-nervous evaluation. It was playing at a small theater in a shopping center near our home, and we felt as if we had never seen the movie before. Michelle and I laughed almost continuously through the film. It was great.

Bull Durham would become a classic sports film. That year Ron Shelton's screenplay was nominated for an Academy Award, and it was selected best original screenplay of 1988 by both the New York Film Critics and the Writers Guild of America. In 2003 *Sports Illustrated* voted it the "Greatest Sports Movie" of all-time, and in 2007 Rotten Tomatoes named it the "Top Sports Movie."

Many point to *Bull Durham* as the reason for the Bulls' success. The franchise was doing extremely well before the release and was one of the top minor league clubs in the country. However, the movie increased attendance beyond capacity and often made the ballpark difficult to manage. Concessions stands and bathrooms had been added over the years, but these facilities were now inadequate with the growing crowds. Almost every night fans sat on the grassy bank behind the left-field wall with the grandstand and bleacher seating full. The push for a new ballpark started at this time as city officials realized the inadequacies of the old park. Raleigh's push for a team also gained steam, and Durham wanted to protect the Bulls.

One of the many positive developments from *Bull Durham* was the increase in souvenir sales. The year prior to the movie, souvenir sales were around $50,000 in t-shirts, hats, and other paraphernalia, not a bad figure for a minor league team. Within the next two years the team was doing over $500,000 a year in sales. The internet was not part of daily life, and online sales were obviously non-existent. The Bulls rented a store in the main mall in the city as an outlet for Bulls' gear, and a 1–800 number was installed to take care of telephone sales. Every male wanted to look like Kevin Costner. Nationally, the movie introduced minor league baseball to a portion of the public that never knew it existed, and with national awareness of this niche industry, values of franchises started to rise as investors realized that money could be made in the sport.

7

"You Want to Buy the Bulls?"

Success often brings competitors, and the Bulls' success was now being viewed in Raleigh with some amount of envy. Raleigh had been a charter member of the Carolina League in 1945, but the capital city had limited success in the league and ultimately the franchise went belly-up in 1967. The Durham Bulls were also struggling during the late '60s and from 1968 to 1971 the Durham franchise played half its games in Raleigh, renamed as the Raleigh-Durham Mets, then the Phillies and finally the Triangles. The Raleigh baseball park was the wonderfully named Devereaux Meadow, but the name was the only appealing aspect of the facility. The creaky stadium seating 5,000 was in an industrial area alongside a major highway, and in 1977 the city tore down the structure to make room for parking for garbage trucks.

The initial success of the Bulls was a purely Durham phenomenon, but by 1983, Raleigh discovered the Bulls, and many fans from that city would make the 20-mile drive to view the games. The *News & Observer*, Raleigh's daily newspaper, began sending a reporter to cover the games, and the three major TV stations for the market covered the team regularly. The Bulls' continued rise in attendance was due in large part to the fact that the team had become a regional attraction.

The city of Raleigh viewed Durham as the weak sister of the Triangle region and began its own plans for a new stadium. A local businessman, Steve Bryant, pushed these plans, and he purchased a Double-A team in Columbus, Georgia, for the purpose of moving it to Raleigh. I viewed these efforts with much alarm. I had developed a successful team that was a regional draw. If Raleigh obtained a team at a higher level than the Single-A Carolina League, the media for the region, which was centered in Raleigh, would undoubtedly desert the Bulls for the new team. Our market would be limited to only Durham. I began discussions with Raleigh city officials about the possibility of perhaps moving the Kinston team in the Carolina League to Raleigh, but they were

7. "You Want to Buy the Bulls?"

intent on having the dominant team and continued to back the efforts of Bryant to move his Southern League team there.

Professional baseball has territorial rules in place to protect franchises and their markets. The territorial rules for minor league baseball at that time stated that no team's city limits could intrude within ten miles of the city limits of another team. When the Raleigh battle began around 1986, the territorial rules for minor league baseball had been written in the 1940s before interstate highways, television, and the growth of metropolitan cities with suburbs that were outside these limits. The city limits of Durham and the city limits of Raleigh came close to the ten-mile restriction, but it remained an open question. Hearings were held with the minor league governing body, lawyers were hired and legal threats were made. The bottom line remained: the Bulls needed protection.

The fight over the Bulls' territory came to a head at the baseball Winter Meetings where amendments to the rules are considered annually. Politics were not my strong suit, but I began a lobbying effort to change the territorial rules. My proposal was that protection needed to be 35 miles from home plate to home plate. City limits were so varied across the country that there was no fairness in a rule that used these limits. Thirty-five miles effectively protected a club for fans who lived within a 30-minute drive to the ballpark. Fortunately, most club owners realized that the new rule would give their clubs much stronger protection. The vote passed. Ultimately, the Columbus, Georgia, club was moved to Zebulon, North Carolina, 36 miles from Durham. Raleigh fans on the east side of that city could go to Zebulon, but for most Raleigh fans, the Bulls remained the dominant and favored team in the market.

Raleigh's efforts to obtain a team opened eyes in Durham. The capital city had proposed spending millions on a ballpark. Durham city officials saw this and began to appreciate what the Bulls were doing for their city. At the same time, crowds were getting so large that Durham Athletic Park could barely handle the overflow. Bathrooms, concessions, parking, and seating continued to be inadequate. When I first brought back the team to Durham, I pushed the phrase "Historic" Durham Athletic Park. "Historic" was a polite way of saying "old," but it helped to obscure the inadequacies of the facility. The reality was that the ballpark was starting to fall apart. Underneath the stands one could reach up and, with bare hands, pull down crumbling concrete and rusting rebar. With the push from Raleigh, Durham city fathers sent architects

There's a Bulldozer on Home Plate

Cartoon by John Cole of the *Durham Morning Herald*. The fight for baseball territorial rights of the Durham-Raleigh market was heated, and the Durham newspaper editorial cartoons provided a Durham perspective.

to the DAP to study the cost of bringing the stadium to modern standards. The cost estimates always pointed to a new stadium as the most cost-efficient way to keep baseball healthy.

Momentum gathered for a new stadium, and plans were developed for a new Bulls ballpark. The prestigious stadium architecture firm HOK was hired to design the stadium and a downtown site was chosen next to the old American Tobacco complex. An automobile dealership located on that site was prepared to move. The American factory had one million square feet of empty space, and firms caught in the excitement of a new Durham made strong commitments to a new downtown redevelopment. The drug company Glaxo was prepared to lease a major portion of the American buildings, and Duke University committed to coming on board.

Financing of the stadium was set with something called tax increment financing with no need for a referendum. Everything appeared to be in order for the Bulls to be playing in a new stadium in 1991. Unfortunately, things are never that easy, and political leaders started to waffle. As with almost all ballpark projects, opposition surfaced. Strong

7. "You Want to Buy the Bulls?"

Cartoon by VC Rogers, *Durham Morning Herald*. Another view of the Durham-Raleigh baseball territorial fight. Durham, which was considered by Raleigh observers as the lesser of the cities in the Raleigh-Durham-Chapel Hill market, took delight in poking fun at Raleigh's failed attempt to invade Durham's territory.

political leadership should have moved forward on a project that was this positive for the city, but in Durham the city council started listening to the naysayers. The council felt they needed cover and decided a public referendum was the safe way to deflect any political negativity. I knew the reality. We were dead in the water, even though civic leaders promised they could bring out the vote and build a winning campaign.

The campaign for the new stadium was intense. The public was voting on a $7 million bond issue, and the opposition raised objections that really had no relevance. It argued that the money should go to schools, even though the funding for schools came from an entirely different funding mechanism. Many argued that the Bulls were doing well enough in the old ballpark, and why did the team need a new facility? A Raleigh television executive, Jim Goodmon, took out full-page ads in

There's a Bulldozer on Home Plate

the Durham newspapers urging voters not to support the referendum. He argued that because the Bulls were really a regional team, a new stadium should be placed somewhere near the airport where it would be convenient to all Triangle residents. He was prepared to help fund a portion of the stadium costs if a regional location could be set.

A victory party was planned at a local restaurant on the election night but there was little confidence in or enthusiasm for the event. I was drained from all the efforts. As results came in, a pall-like silence fell on the attendees. It was clear that the new stadium was dead. Because of the controversy over the ballpark, turnout for the election was huge, and the referendum failed by a significant margin. We drank a few beers at the restaurant, but there was little joy. Everyone left quickly after the final results were announced. Six months later, Durham had a $100-million referendum on infrastructure and other needs in the city. Fewer than half the voters that voted in the stadium referendum cast their ballots for the measure that passed.

The future of the Bulls was now in doubt. I had made the most of Durham Athletic Park over the ten years of ownership of the franchise, but the DAP was falling apart and could not be home to a professional franchise for the long term. This was the livelihood for my family, and it was time to get out. The week after the referendum, I received a phone call from Jim Goodmon, the TV executive. He wanted to meet and discuss how to develop his proposal for a new regional stadium. The thought did not excite me. Durham was home. I had fought for the Bulls to stay in Durham and could not see moving the Bulls out of the city.

I met with Goodmon for lunch. He began talking about a regional stadium, but I stopped him. I told him that I was tired of political battles and could not see moving the team. However, if he wanted to buy the team, it was for sale. If he owned the team, he could do whatever he wished. Goodmon hesitated. He had not expected that the team was for sale. He asked for a price, and I gave the figure of $4 million. He replied that if the financials for the team justified this, he would consider buying the team. A week later, he accepted the offer.

Lawyers never make things easy, but by the spring of the next year, everything was signed and the deal completed. I was no longer owner of the Durham Bulls. When the news of the sale hit the media, city officials were shocked. They had never believed that I would sell, and the real prospect of losing the Bulls hit them in the face. An executive from Raleigh was now the owner, and his proposal was that the team would move. Now, one of the gems of the city was about to leave. Where

7. "You Want to Buy the Bulls?"

the council had hesitated with me, there was no hesitation with Jim Goodmon. The Bulls had to be kept. The team could not move. Within months, plans for a new ballpark on a different downtown Durham site were presented. The cost of this new stadium was more than double what had been in the original plans, but it passed with no need for a referendum. Goodmon, who had been serious on his regional site, saw the community come together to keep the Bulls, and he accepted the new proposal. He had the deep pockets to make these plans work, and his organization became the developer for the massive American Tobacco property. He would later build office buildings surrounding the stadium, and the area became the centerpiece of Durham's revival.

With the loss in the referendum, I saw few positive options, and it was a low period for me. In retrospect, the loss was a significantly positive event for all involved. Jim Goodmon had the financial resources to make a new stadium work. In a few years he purchased a Triple-A franchise and the Durham Bulls became one of the top franchises in all of minor league baseball. The team was a national phenomenon, and crowds averaged a half million in attendance each year. As a developer, the American Tobacco project set Durham on a significant upward growth spiral. Downtown Durham came alive and the city became the hottest market in the Triangle. The *New York Times* in one of its lists named Durham one of the top fifty cities in the world.

As for me, it was the best outcome that could have happened. At the time, I did not feel it, but with my share of the sales price, my family was financially in a positive position. Now there were resources to develop other projects. The sale of the Bulls did not include a sale of the Burlington baseball club or *Baseball America*, and these businesses were solid and remained part of my organization. The initial stockholders who had invested in the team received their first payout. The investors had received no dividends in the first eleven years and had been patient and let me use funds for other teams and investments. Now they had a significant return on investment and would continue to receive payouts over the next 30 years.

In reality, the sale was the best for the Bulls. My strength was in start-ups. For ten years I had made do in the old park. With a new stadium on the horizon, the organization needed to grow. Without the funds from the sale, I might not have been able to make the upgrades and additions that a new stadium would need. I certainly would not have been able to purchase a Triple-A club and build office towers. Jim Goodmon was able to do everything in a first-class manner. The Bulls prospered.

8

"What's That Round Piece of Rubber For?"

In 1991 after the sale of the Bulls, I had the resources to purchase an expansion minor-league ice hockey franchise in the East Coast Hockey League (ECHL). It was a gamble. No coliseum or arena existed in the Raleigh-Durham area equipped to supply a sheet of ice suitable for professional hockey. However, a possibility existed at an older facility, Dorton Arena, built in the 1950s and located on the state fairgrounds in Raleigh. The fairgrounds management had an interest in renting the facility for minor league hockey if ice was possible in the old building. The team would be responsible for purchasing and installing the ice-making equipment. The arena, with a seating capacity of around 5,000, was the right size for a minor league hockey club, and investigations into ice systems led us to acquire a mat system that could be placed on the concrete flooring to make ice. It was not ideal, but financially it made sense. The organization was now in the hockey business.

I hired Pete Bock, the first GM of the Bulls, to run this new venture. Pete had left the Bulls after the first two years when the Hawaii Islanders of the Triple-A Pacific Coast League hired him to run that operation. Pete was in Hawaii for five years but wanted to come back to North Carolina. Originally, I brought Pete back to supervise the baseball interests when the movie was being shot, and he was available when the hockey opportunity arose. It was a stretch for Pete as his knowledge of hockey was less than mine. I had actually seen a game. But I knew Pete could run a good sports operation, and he was eager to take on the project.

The National Hockey League (NHL) has no need for an extensive farm system. In contrast, baseball needs four or five levels to develop players for the big leagues. NHL teams traditionally have only one farm team, usually in the American Hockey League (AHL). Major League Baseball subsidizes the minors by paying salaries and most other player

8. *"What's That Round Piece of Rubber For?"*

expenses. However, as we moved forward with the hockey team, we knew we would have to pay salaries, workers' compensation, and equipment for the players. These were expenses we had never experienced in baseball.

One of the deciding factors that helped sway the decision to go into hockey came from the owner of the Hampton Roads (Norfolk, Virginia) hockey team that had been a member of the ECHL for just a few seasons. The owner was a former baseball executive, and he encouraged us. "It's just the same as running a minor league baseball club," he told us. "And there are fewer games." Pete and I questioned him on how to acquire players. He laughed. "You don't need to know anything about hockey or players. Just hire a good coach who knows the game and he will take care of all of that." As for the extra costs, he explained that financially it was doable. Tickets for minor league hockey games were higher than minor league baseball tickets. Plus, he emphasized, there were no rainouts in hockey.

The ECHL had only been in existence for a few years, and it was starting to grow. Hockey was entering Southern markets that were not usually considered hockey territory, and interest was rising in the sport. The league wanted to be in the Raleigh-Durham market and welcomed our application. Most importantly, the price was right. For $50,000 we could obtain a franchise.

We named the club the Raleigh IceCaps. The baseball team had been the Raleigh Capitals and Caps. With the announcement that hockey was coming to Raleigh, the public showed immediate interest. The Triangle had experienced a large population growth in the prior decade with many Northerners and Canadians moving to the region. A number of these folks had been hockey fans. We also found that minor league baseball fans often made hockey their winter sport, and stock car racing fans and wrestling fans seemed to like the occasional brawl. One person who did not seem to appreciate hockey was the local sports editor. He knew nothing about the sport and assumed it would fail. Pete Bock took a puck to his office to show him what the little round piece of hard rubber looked like. He assigned the golf writer to cover the team, reportedly because he wanted that writer to quit. But interest became so great that the *News & Observer* had to give more coverage than they had planned, and the golf writer never quit.

It also turned out that the local ticket scalpers loved the team. The IceCaps become the hottest sports ticket in the market. Most weekend games were sold out, and one scalper confided that he made more

There's a Bulldozer on Home Plate

Dorton Arena (above and right). Located in Raleigh, North Carolina, on the State Fairgrounds, Dorton Arena opened in 1952. It is owned by the State of North Carolina and has been designated as a National Historic Civil Engineering Landmark for its unique design. The arena was home to the Raleigh IceCaps of the ECHL from 1991 to 1998.

money on some IceCaps games than he made on Duke vs. Carolina basketball matchups.

    At that same time, North Carolina State University was beginning the process of planning for a new basketball-only arena to replace the aging Reynolds Coliseum. ACC basketball was the number-one sport in the state, and N.C. State's national championship in 1983 had made the team a major draw. When athletic officials at the university saw the interest and attendance at IceCaps games, they became interested in making hockey a potential tenant of the new building. Adding 35 hockey dates to the event schedule could be financially beneficial for the new facility. Pete and I began negotiations with the athletic department and met with the architects to plan on including hockey as part of the design. Good progress was made and excitement was rising about the prospect of a new larger facility for the IceCaps, when almost all contact with the university stopped. Phone calls to the athletic department were met with vague assurances that it would get back in touch when plans were further along.

8. "What's That Round Piece of Rubber For?"

A few months later I received a phone call from an individual informing me that he was the campaign finance director for the governor of North Carolina. He stated that he was going to help me move to Fayetteville. I was confused at first, for I had no desire to move to Fayetteville, but he cleared things up when he let me know that it was the IceCaps that were going to move to a new arena in Fayetteville. He told me that an AHL team would be moving to the new N.C. State arena, and he wanted to make certain the IceCaps had a place to move. For four years we had worked to make hockey a viable sport in the Triangle, and I let the caller know that we were not interested in moving.

Baseball rules protect a club's home territory (see: 35-mile rule), and no baseball team can move to another's territory without compensation. Hockey has no rules to protect the territory of minor league clubs, and it was apparent that we were being pushed out. Politics had never been my chosen field, and I had no desire to be involved in a fight with a group tied to the governor. However, another group from Winston-Salem had an interest in purchasing the IceCaps. The group was headed by the son of a former United States senator. It assured me it could obtain the AHL franchise and place it in the new Raleigh arena. In the meantime, it would continue to operate the IceCaps and then move the ECHL team to another market when the new arena was ready. With a fight looming between the governor and the senator, it was a situation I needed to avoid. I quickly sold the Raleigh IceCaps to the Winston-Salem group.

There's a Bulldozer on Home Plate

As luck would have it, neither group obtained a lease. The National Hockey League became aware of the potential of a new 18,000 seat arena, and ultimately the Hartford Whalers moved south and became the successful Carolina Hurricanes. While the situation was uncomfortable for a period, the Raleigh IceCaps had four glorious years. We were successful and set the stage for major league sports to come to the Triangle. We proved there was a market for the sport. Without the IceCaps, North Carolina State University would not have changed its plans for a basketball-only arena and ice would not have been part of the architectural plans. The sale price of the IceCaps was around $2 million, a positive return on the original investment for the franchise and $200,000 for the ice system for Dorton Arena.

Hockey was a great learning experience. Most importantly, I learned that it was possible to operate an independent team in a sport in which I had little knowledge. Certainly, if I could run a successful independent hockey team, an independent baseball league should be possible. It was time to move forward on a new baseball league.

But there were other things to learn—the fun things that made the venture into hockey a rewarding experience. I learned that pucks are hard and come from Czechoslovakia. I learned that the ice is painted white. I had always thought that the ice was naturally white and was shocked when I received an invoice for white ice paint. I learned that there are used Zamboni dealers. Zamboni ice resurfacers are expensive machines and I was amazed to find that firms actually deal in used Zambonis.

Dorton Arena made for other gains in knowledge. Specifically, glass buildings are not ideal for hockey. When the Dorton Arena was constructed in the early 1950s, it was a significant architectural achievement, built in an elliptical shape with glass walls surrounding the seats and playing surface. When spring and daylight savings came, the sun would not have set for the 7 p.m. games. One goal faced west and our team always tried to arrange for the visiting goalie to be facing the sun. This was not viewed with satisfaction by the opposing team, and the league office sent us stern letters. Also, cow washing pits are not usually a part of the sport of hockey. Dorton was built for the yearly agricultural fair with a cow washing pit at one entrance. This proved difficult to explain to hockey fans. Part of the learning experience was that a good air conditioning system was needed for hockey arenas. Unfortunately, this was not part of the Dorton Arena infrastructure. The air conditioning system was minimal and on warm spring nights, fog rose from the

8. "What's That Round Piece of Rubber For?"

melting ice. The game would be stopped and our players skated around the ice waving towels, trying to push the fog away.

Finally, I learned that while the difference between athletes is slight, hockey players have an edge on baseball players in their post-game attire. I was accustomed to baseball players whose usual post-game look featured a t-shirt, shorts, flip-flops, and tobacco juice running down their chins. Hockey players, who have been smashing each other against the boards with an occasional round of fisticuffs, wear coats and ties after their matches and look like members of the Junior Chamber of Commerce. It was always an amazing transformation.

For my family, owning a hockey team was a positive experience. Michelle, from Northern Maine, had always enjoyed the sport, and she loved coming to the games. Shy Claire, a polite little girl, decided that the fights were her favorite thing, and she would pound on the glass as the players pounded each other on the ice. And for Hoffman, it was the beginning of a love affair with the sport.

The Deep End of Adulthood
by Hoffman Wolff

When I was in elementary school in the early 1990s, my dad owned the local minor-league hockey team. I know what you're probably thinking: "Having your dad own the local minor-league hockey team must have been awesome." In reality: Yeah. It was.

My dad started the team when I was seven. In hindsight, starting a hockey team in North Carolina, especially before the NHL started putting teams in unintuitive places like Nashville and Phoenix, was sort of an odd idea. (My dad had a lot of odd ideas. A few years later, he would move our family to Quebec City to start a baseball club. Another time, he proposed a family spring break trip to Narcos-era Colombia so he could see about starting a league there, which my mom quickly vetoed.)

It was odder still because my North Carolina-bred father had spent his career in baseball and didn't actually know anything about hockey. But one of his baseball cohorts had recently started an inexplicably but wildly popular hockey team in Norfolk, Va., and apparently other people were making money running teams in places like Richmond, Knoxville and Louisville, so he went out and bought an East Coast Hockey League franchise for Raleigh.

The team was christened the "IceCaps," after Raleigh's old minor-league baseball team, the Capitals. My dad and his general manager, another baseball guy named Pete Bock, sketched out their idea for the logo, which looks like something that two middle-aged guys with no particular design flair would think up: the state Capitol's rotunda floating above the word "ICECAPS."

There's a Bulldozer on Home Plate

Unsurprisingly, the Raleigh area didn't really have a suitable hockey venue. The team ended up shoehorning a rink into Dorton Arena, a 1950s-era fairgrounds barn which typically hosted livestock shows and obscure wrestling events. Its architects designed it with hockey in mind in the same way Yankee Stadium was designed with NASCAR in mind: that is, not even remotely. Its most glaring design flaw: its exterior walls were made of glass, which caused problems when facing errant 90-MPH snapshots.

There were other issues to work through and potential red flags, from Zambonis (Do you just call somewhere and order one? Does anyone in Raleigh know how to drive one?) to local news coverage, as none of the area's sports media people knew anything about the game, either. Shortly before the first season, Pete stopped by the local newspaper's office to bring a puck to the sports editor—he had never seen one up close.

Improbably, the arena and the team and the whole thing worked. The team was pretty good; the place sold out on a regular basis; and I fell in love with the blue-and-silver-clad IceCaps, led by a magnificently-named forward from Ontario named Lyle Wildgoose. Hockey novices or not, my family religiously followed the ups and downs of the team. The games were broadcast on a shaky AM radio station whose signal died about a mile from our house, and during the third period of road games, my dad often drove to a nearby McDonald's where the signal could be picked up, ordered a sundae, and sat in the car and nervously listened as the IceCaps tried to hold off the Erie Panthers or Winston-Salem Thunderbirds.

Despite the fact that I didn't actually play hockey (barely anyone in North Carolina did), my position as the authority of this strange new sport was cemented at Durham Academy Lower School, and my ego was boosted when random students would walk up to tell me that they had been at last night's game.

Furthermore, as a kid obsessed with logos and uniforms, the East Coast Hockey League now brought to my attention 15 more teams' worth of fascinating, sometimes politically-incorrect designs featuring teal, lightning bolts, stick-wielding natives and skating frogs. In the pre-internet age, a previously-unseen opposing team coming to town was exciting: all I knew about a team's visual identity came from the small black-and-white logos in the IceCaps' game program, so even their uniform colors would be a surprise: "Huh, look at that, the Dayton Bombers are blue and gold. I had them pegged as red and black, or maybe green."

Having grown up around minor-league baseball, I was accustomed to the languid nature of the ballpark that meshed with my polite Episcopalian upbringing: elderly couples keeping score, mascots wandering around patting children on the head, and appreciative but unfrenzied applause for good defensive plays and clutch hits. Beer was available, but rarely consumed to excess. I was also familiar with the atmosphere at Duke and UNC college basketball games, where they didn't even sell beer. For the moneyed

8. "What's That Round Piece of Rubber For?"

alumni who made up most of the crowd, you sat smugly when your team won and tsk-tsked the next day at the country club on the rare occasions when it didn't. Harassing the opposing team was left to the students.

The often-charged environment of a hockey arena, as well as the more freewheeling nature of the sport's fans, created a slightly adult thrill that was new to me. Now I was spending winter evenings in Dorton Arena's red wooden seats, surrounded by large groups of grown-ups chanting "you suck!" at opposing goaltenders. IceCaps fans, while generally good-natured, drank liberally, cursed freely and gave the finger to opposing players in the penalty box. I quickly got used to making my way through a haze of cigarette smoke in Dorton Arena's dingy concourse between periods, navigating around spilled beers and men (and women) dropping f-bombs.

Also, the players fought. I occasionally encounter people unfamiliar with hockey who assume that the fights are some pushing and shoving that is broken up quickly by referees, like you might see in a skirmish at a basketball or football game. It's not that. It's two guys trying to beat the crap out of each other while everyone else on the ice and in the crowd stands and watches and cheers. It's brutal and bloody and it can sometimes be frightening. But the primal nature of the fights and the crowd's reactions also added to the "so that's what grown-up land is like" adventure of being at the arena.

Another contrast between the IceCaps and our local Class-A baseball team was the players themselves. The ballplayers were nervous 22-year-olds taught to keep quiet and follow orders (in the baseball world, possessing a discernible personality is often seen as a "character issue" that can harm chances at a promotion to higher levels). Teams were managed by stoic, gum-chomping organization men named Larry or Mel whose job was to quickly determine who should be moved up to Double-A and who should be let go in order to make room for next season's crop of equally colorless recruits. The teams visiting the Bulls were interchangeable and anonymous, and none of their players stayed around long enough for opposing fans to know or care who they were.

In contrast, the ECHL consisted mostly of guys whose NHL window had mostly closed; as a consequence, they seemed to decide that, what the hell, they might as well actually try to enjoy themselves and let their "hockey hair" grow another inch or two while they were at it. Teams' head coaches were their own special breed of hockey mavericks and lifers, such as John Brophy, a white-haired lunatic who wore bolo ties and attacked opposing coaches during games, or Doug Sauter, who looked like Yosemite Sam's brother and about whom there is a news report on the internet entitled "Coach Stops Runaway Horse by Biting Ear." The IceCaps broke the mold by hiring a reasonably normal human being as their coach: a young, collected Minnesotan named Kurt Kleinendorst whom I remember coming to our house for a barbecue and shooting hoops in the driveway. I have no idea how my father and Pete ended

There's a Bulldozer on Home Plate

up selecting him, as it's not like they knew anything about how to choose a hockey coach, but he's still coaching professionally today.

Unlike in baseball, ECHL teams weren't very concerned with moving their players to higher levels, so guys could stay on the same team for several seasons. Because of the more colorful, long-lasting players and coaches, fierce rivalries were found throughout the league, felt by both players and fans. On weekend nights, dozens of opposing fans would travel for their teams' games at Dorton and return the favor by yelling profane things at IceCaps players. Raleigh fans reserved an extra level of contempt for their rival from down Interstate 40, the Greensboro Monarchs. Their best player was a gloriously hateable right winger named Phil Berger, who wore an earring and a permanent smirk, resumed skating before the national anthem finished playing, and reveled in returning IceCaps fans' outstretched middle fingers. 25 years later, I have rooted against various other teams and players throughout my life as a sports fan, but my disdain for a team will never reach the heights of the utter loathing I felt towards the Monarchs as an 8 year old.

We would also travel to some IceCaps road games, played in a hodgepodge of municipal civic centers and athletic complexes that varied widely in size and professionalism. Greensboro's home was an enormous coliseum where they turned out the arena lights and played "Welcome to the Jungle" during pregame player introductions. I jealously admitted to myself that seeing the spotlighted Monarchs hit the ice as Axl Rose's opening riff blasted was pretty damn cool. On the other end of the spectrum, in a suburb of Roanoke, Va., the home team played in a weird little hybrid ice rink/workout facility where you could see people jogging on treadmills as the game was going on. My dad would give a polite "hello" to other traveling IceCaps fans, who typically sat in a section together, but we would always sit in another part of the arena to avoid being put in the impolite situation of having to join in and tell the Charlotte Checkers' goalie that he sucked, as correct as this assessment may have been.

For two seasons when I was 10 and 11 years old, I was the radio guy's statistician. The team's broadcaster was a kind, good-humored vagabond named Andy Young who called baseball games in Montana or Alaska or somewhere during the summer and returned in time for the IceCaps season. He needed someone to keep track of goal and penalty announcements, as hockey's faster pace doesn't always give the broadcaster enough time to jot everything down. (Actually, I don't know if this is true. I've never sat with any other hockey broadcasters, so maybe there was plenty of time for him to write everything, and he was just doing my dad a favor by inviting me up there.) Whatever the case, I dutifully noted every "14:56 2ND—RAL—PEREIRA—2:00 HOOKING," sitting between Andy and the "color commentator," who was whichever IceCaps player happened to be injured and not playing that night. At every return from a commercial break, listeners would unfailingly hear "Welcome

8. "What's That Round Piece of Rubber For?"

back to Goodberry's Frozen Custard IceCaps hockey, with Andy Young, injured forward Frank Cirone and statistician Hoffman Wolff."

Of course, it didn't last. Magic never does. The novelty of the team wore off, crowds dwindled, and my classmates asked about the team less and less. My dad sold the team, and Andy took a year-round job with a team in Maine, and I grew up. I sometimes wish that, as an adult, I could have just one more season with the IceCaps, but I don't think it would be the same. For me, part of the IceCaps experience was being a kid around adults in an unsanitized, not-totally-family-friendly setting. Now that I'm one of those adults, it's just a game, and beer and cigarettes aren't mysterious, and taunting a minor-league hockey player seems kind of lame, and I have other stuff going on. But I hope in the near future my son has a Lyle Wildgoose to cheer for and a Phil Berger to root against, and gets little tastes of the grown-up world, like walking on his own through a hazy, boozy arena concourse to buy nachos and a Sprite, before being thrown into the deep end of adulthood.

9

Where in the Hell Is Thunder Bay?

The IceCaps were an important step as an introduction to independent baseball. The ECHL was effectively an independent league, receiving no help from the NHL. The more I thought about it, the more I became convinced it was time to do something with an independent baseball league. Success had come in a sport I knew nothing about. Why couldn't success happen with independent baseball? It was time to stop dreaming.

By the 1990s, minor league teams were generating significantly more income than ever before. With the advent of sports administration programs, better-prepared candidates were applying to the sport. In the 1970s, cities actively worked against minor league baseball coming to their communities. By the 1990s, municipalities were welcoming the bush leagues. Cities planned state-of-the-art facilities to attract minor league teams. The minor leagues were hot. In 1988 Buffalo opened a new state-of-the-art facility that drew over a million fans, a remarkable figure, and continued to draw over a million fans for the next six years. Downtown revitalization was accompanying these new stadiums, and cities were excited about the potential of a minor league team. Even at the independent level, several municipalities such as Salt Lake City and Portland demonstrated that an independent team could work in the right market with the right ownership.

Thus began the search for sites. I traveled to Florida, a state with many baseball facilities. Could this be a potential area for a league? But Florida had major league spring training and little enthusiasm could be generated for bringing a new minor league to the area. At one point I started driving to South Texas. A new independent league, the Lone Star League, had started in that area, and I was eager to jump on board. But by the time I reached Mississippi, the league folded and I turned around and returned. In 1950, North Carolina had 45 minor league

9. Where in the Hell Is Thunder Bay?

teams. By the late 1970s the state was down to four teams. Surely, potential must still exist in the state, but as I toured the old parks and examined the markets, it was clear that the ballparks were too run-down and the markets too small to support a league without the major leagues paying the salaries. Was a new league really possible?

Then, out of the blue, phone calls from individuals in the Upper Midwest reached my desk at *Baseball America*, which had taken over the readership of the hardcore baseball fan who had previously read *The Sporting News*. This little newspaper now was now seen as the source for all things baseball. Phone calls from fans and subscribers were usually handled by the staff, but sometimes the strange phone calls were routed to me. In a period of a couple months in early 1991 I received phone calls from individuals in Duluth, Minnesota; Sioux Falls, South Dakota; and Thunder Bay, Ontario, asking how their cities could get minor league baseball.

It was strange. Why were individuals in this geographic area pushing for a return of minor league baseball? How was I to respond? My initial answer to these inquiries was that there was probably no possibility for their cities to ever get a team. No minor league existed in that area of the country, and the major leagues were certainly not going to add any new cities to the farm systems. But for each of the calls, I took the name and phone number and let them know that if anything developed, I would be back in touch.

The call from Thunder Bay caused me to scramble. I had never heard of that city, and I prided myself on my knowledge of geography. As the caller chatted on about his city, I quickly took out a road atlas to see where in the hell Thunder Bay was. Earlier, a call had come from Duluth, and looking at the map, I could see that the Canadian city was just about three and a half hours north of Duluth. The caller informed me that the city had a stadium, and good baseball interest existed. The area's population was over 100,000. This was positive. With Sioux Falls also looking for a team, could this be the area to start an independent league?

With little knowledge of the Upper Midwest, it was time to learn. An old Class C League, the Northern League, had been fairly successful in the 1940s and 1950s. However, by the early 1970s, the league was dead, and no professional baseball had been played in the area for over two decades. What could be done and were there any adequate facilities still left? Three phone calls did not make a league, but maybe something was there. It wouldn't hurt to take a couple of days off, fly into

There's a Bulldozer on Home Plate

Minneapolis–St. Paul, rent a car, and explore the area. Looking at old ballparks was a quiet passion, and luck has been good to me in recent years. Maybe I could find six cities and start a league. It was a nice little dream.

I telephoned the three callers. They were surprised to hear from me, but meetings were set and they were urged to contact city officials. Was there any chance for baseball to return to these cities? Duluth and Sioux Falls had been members of the original Northern League, and some portions of those ballparks were still standing. The drive from the Minneapolis–St. Paul airport to Duluth was a little over three hours, and as the car rose over the crest of a hill, Duluth and Lake Superior spread out below. For me, it was an impressive and exciting view, bringing back memories from 20 years before when I drove over a large green bridge into Savannah. I had left home in Durham in early April to start exploring cities. The azaleas were in bloom in North Carolina. Duluth was still in the last stages of winter, with huge sheets of ice floating on Lake Superior.

Duluth prospered in the early 20th century and was a major port for the mining industry. The architecture of many of the main buildings in the city was early 20th century, with massive stone structures that showed the confidence of a city on the make. But mining declined in the latter half of the 20th century, and Duluth struggled. The city was now positioning itself as a summer tourist site, with walkways along Lake Superior, some newer hotels, and a redeveloped entertainment district in the downtown.

Unfortunately, redevelopment had not reached the ballpark. The stadium, sitting behind a bowling alley, was on the edge of a modest neighborhood. A 1938 WPA project, the outside walls were made of paving blocks that had been taken out of the city streets in the 1930s to build the stadium. The covered grandstand had a capacity of approximately 2,500, and with room for bleachers on either side, capacity could probably be stretched to around 4,000. But it had been 20 years since a team had made its home at Wade Stadium, and the facility was a wondrous wreck. At the stadium main entrance where fans no longer entered and boarded-up concessions counters stood unready to serve, I viewed a concourse surface that had originally been smooth concrete. It was no longer such. Over the years, the frigid Duluth winters had caused the concrete to buckle and heave, and the concourse had turned to a hazardous maze as I maneuvered around bulging concrete blocks that made pedestrian traffic a difficult journey. I passed through the

9. Where in the Hell Is Thunder Bay?

stairways to the field and stared at light towers that had few working fixtures with no one willing or needed to climb the rusted steel spans to replace the bulbs in the outdated lighting plant. The grandstand was full of bird droppings with gulls the only creatures left to watch the empty field. The barren playing surface had a few solitary blades of grass trying to peek through the formerly frozen turf.

I was not deterred. The ballpark just smelled of baseball. I fantasized that with work, "The Wade," as it was known, could be made ready. If someone would buy into the dream, the ballpark could come alive. Yes, the lights certainly needed upgrading, the field needed grass, and the seating with splintering wooden benches needed painting. The concourse would have to be torn up and replaced with new concrete. Certainly, the interior wiring would not be enough to support the needs of a modern baseball operation. But if the city could see the potential, if I could sell the vision, Wade Stadium would be a special place. I knew I wanted to bring a team to the Duluth-Superior market. Meetings with city officials gave some hope.

It's important for a minor league team to have a history. A team may fold, but good memories remain. In reviving a team, it is important to be able to play off the memories. This northern Minnesota area had a good baseball history. From 1934 through 1970, except for the World War II years, Duluth had a team. And even during that war, the unique, professional Class E Twin Ports League was formed but did not last the season.

Across the harbor was the city of Superior, Wisconsin (motto: "Next to Duluth, we're Superior"). Superior also had a team for many years, and in 1955 when the Superior Blues folded, the Dukes became the Duluth-Superior Dukes. For many seasons the Detroit Tigers supplied the players, and Denny McClain, Bill Freehan, Willie Horton, and dozens of other future big leaguers began their careers playing for the Duluth-Superior Dukes. And the fans in Duluth remembered.

With the rush of finding a ballpark that might work, I headed north to Thunder Bay. It was a stunning drive along the shore of Lake Superior, and over the years, it would be a favorite trip. Throughout the Upper Midwest, I found other great drives. Driving through Iowa was amazing with the spectacularly endless fields of corn, but for me Lake Superior always beat corn.

Thunder Bay was originally two sister cities, Port Arthur and Fort William. The two cities merged in the 1970s. At one point Fort William did have a baseball team, from 1914 to 1916 in an older version of

There's a Bulldozer on Home Plate

Port Arthur Stadium, Thunder Bay, Ontario. Originally built for amateur baseball in the 1950s, Port Arthur Stadium was home of the Thunder Bay Whiskey Jacks from 1993 to 1998. In the early years of the team, the citizens flocked to the ballpark with crowds spilling onto the outfield warning track. But new ownership was looking for a larger market, and in 1999 the team was moved to a new stadium in Schaumburg, IL.

the Northern League. That ballpark had long since vanished, but in the 1950s, a stadium was built for amateur baseball. Port Arthur Stadium was a sweet little ballpark with a covered grandstand that sat around 2,000 with bleachers down the first base line. The facility was in moderately good shape as amateur baseball was still played there. It could be made ready for minor league ball. I was not expecting this in a city that was previously unknown to me. I met with city officials and there was interest. Was it possible?

9. Where in the Hell Is Thunder Bay?

The drive from Thunder Bay to Sioux Falls was long, but the excitement of two possible ballparks kept me alert. In Sioux Falls, as opposed to the older economies of Duluth and Thunder Bay, I found a modern, booming community. South Dakota's lack of personal and corporate income tax made the area attractive to business. The city was growing, and it had a ballpark. It was built in the early 1960s for the minor league team that played in the Northern League until the league folded in 1971. However, compared to Duluth and Thunder Bay, two facilities that needed extensive upgrades, Sioux Falls Stadium was a disaster. Bringing baseball to the city would be a challenge. The bench seating was no longer attached to the concrete grandstand, and the long wooden seating planks were strewn around the facility like giant pick-up sticks. The stadium had no visiting dressing room and no roof covered the grandstand. Only a few rusting folding chairs remained, disguised as box seats. However, the most negative factor was the American Legion baseball program. The Legion controlled the ballpark and did not want competition.

Over the years, American Legion baseball had been an important part of the amateur baseball scene in the United States. The baseball was primarily for the best high school players in a region. With a national baseball tournament at the end of the summer, Legion baseball was a significant presence across the United States for several decades after World War II. However, by 1990, interest had waned and the programs were often run by World War II veterans who no longer had the interest or energy to keep standards high and facilities in good shape. I had run into Legion programs in other cities in my baseball journeys, and it was always a touchy situation to be in opposition to the Legion. Legionnaires were local, they were war heroes, and they promoted baseball for youth in the city. It was like fighting motherhood and apple pie. I would need to meet with city officials to see if it made sense to take on the American Legion. One local diehard, David Kemp, was pushing the prospect of a return of pro ball, and he introduced me to a councilman who believed it might be possible to find city money to restore the facility. The Legion might be an obstacle, he said, but it could be overcome.

I headed back to Durham with hope growing. I had found three ballparks where there was interest. I had nothing more than this, but still, it might be possible. To start a minor league team in any city is never easy, but to start a completely new league means a considerable number of blocks need to fall into place. No new league had started and survived since 1960. No commitments had been given. Procuring leases in all the cities and dealing with municipal governments is never a speedy or easy process. Elected officials need to be convinced that spending hundreds of thousands of dollars on a phantom league will be a good idea and that it is necessary to bring their stadiums up to professional standards. And where are the owners? Can six or eight minor league operators be persuaded that it makes sense to start a new league with no major league help? And would this work? In the prior 40 years, a few efforts to start baseball leagues without major league affiliations have been tried, but all had failed miserably.

Probably the most important requirement in choosing a minor league locale is population. Are enough people in the market to make a team viable? Professional baseball is a business and it needs people. The goal was to find markets with a minimum area population of 150,000. The three cities visited had populations that were close to that benchmark. But were there three more cities in the geographical area that could support a team and make a league?

The next few months became a time for studying maps, making phone calls and taking early-morning flights from RDU to MSP to try to discover baseball parks. Knowledge of the Midwest grew as I explored Madison, Fargo, Winnipeg, Green Bay, Lacrosse, Waterloo, Bismarck, Rochester, Lincoln, St. Cloud, Eau Claire, Grand Forks, Mankato, Moorhead, and a half-dozen other markets. They all had potential, they all had ballparks, but always a problem existed. Some cities did not believe they needed a minor league team. Others had no money for improvements, and a few cities were actively hostile to the prospect of minor league baseball.

Without enough cities, it was a project that would never happen. Frustration was rising. Then, out of the blue, a friend from minor league baseball called. He had heard of the search. He was working in the ticket department of the NBA's Minnesota Timberwolves, but his baseball interest remained strong. Baseball is always tough to give up. He asked if St. Paul, Minnesota, had been checked out. Minneapolis and St. Paul are the twin cities that sit across from each other on the Mississippi River. It is a major league market, and the Minnesota Twins are its big-league team. Prior to the 1960s when Major League Baseball had only 16 teams and was located primarily in the northeastern quadrant of the U.S., Minneapolis and St. Paul each had minor league teams. The Millers and the Saints played in one of the top minor leagues, the American Association. Both were successful franchises with a great rivalry.

9. Where in the Hell Is Thunder Bay?

Then in 1961 the Washington Senators major league team moved to the market, and minor league baseball was gone.

I knew the minor league history in the market and, most importantly, knew that both of the old minor league ballparks had been torn down. It was a problem I faced in other cities with demolished ballparks. The old park in St. Paul had been called Midway Stadium, and when I let my friend know that without Midway, there was no sense in thinking about St. Paul, he interrupted. "Oh no, they did tear down the old Midway, but they built a new stadium in the 1980s for amateur baseball. It is still called Midway and is good enough for a minor league team."

This was interesting. Did it make sense to go into a major league market and try to compete with a major league team? I continued talking with my friend. Minneapolis had become the glamor city in the area, and St. Paul often felt like the poor stepchild. The major league park, an indoor facility called the Metrodome, was located in Minneapolis, and many St. Paul citizens resented that they had to drive there to see the team. My friend knew that St. Paul citizens had civic pride and believed that the potential was good for a successful minor league team. It was time for a trip to St. Paul. The city was the most positive market I had visited. The ballpark was good, and the city officials were enthusiastic. St. Paul was added to the list of possible cities.

With four cities that seemed ready, it was time to push for the final two members of a league that was getting closer to reality. A trip to Sioux City, a wrong-way drive down the interstate, and a meeting with the mayor made that city a definite possibility. The mayor promised to build a new stadium for the league, but he stipulated one major condition: He would not commit the funds and start construction on a ballpark until the league had five other cities signed and sealed. This could pose a problem.

Winnipeg had been a strong candidate for the fifth slot, but the potential owner, Sam Katz, pulled back, wanting to wait to see if the league would survive. Fargo, North Dakota, had strong interest and ownership was ready. But the ballpark was controlled by the American Legion, and the organization was unwilling to share the facility. St. Cloud, Minnesota, looked to be ideal. The geography for the league was perfect. The ballpark was small but could work, local ownership was ready, and the city had a great history in the Northern League. But the city fathers were not willing to step up. I was down to my final option: Rochester, Minnesota.

Rochester, just 90 miles south of St. Paul, was the home of the

There's a Bulldozer on Home Plate

Mayo Clinic, the world-renowned medical facility. The clinic was also the major industry and employer in the city. Rochester's population was around 70,000, not the 150,000 that a team really needed. But the city did have a compact little ballpark, Mayo Field, with a capacity of around 2,000 fans. The recreation department was willing to lease the facility, but no funds would be available for improvements. The only money the city could allocate to the stadium was for installation of hot water heaters, a definite improvement as players did need to shower after the games. This was not what I had hoped for, but no other options were on the horizon. A commitment was made to Rochester to become the sixth city in the league.

It was time to find ownership. Over the months, several prospective owners had made contact, but it had been too early to bring anyone on board. Now, the time was right and ownership was crucial. The need was for experienced owners who understood independent baseball. The league would fail with weak or unproven management. Very few owners in minor league baseball had experience with the independent game, and the pool of potential candidates was extremely small. Yet almost every owner who had experience with an independent team was eager to hear my pitch. None had made much money running a team without major league help, but the experience of independent baseball was intoxicating. Independent owners were in charge of the team. They hired the manager, set up tryout camps and helped select players, and signed local players who gave the team more identity in the market. Wins and losses mattered, not just the concession gross, and having a team that was really their own was why most owners had gotten in the game in the first place. This was real baseball.

The deal for ownership was simple. No franchise fee would be charged for the first three years. If the league succeeded and the operator wanted to continue, he would then pay $50,000 to me as the commissioner and organizer. At that time, many minor league franchises were being sold for well over $1 million and if the league succeeded, the owners would certainly profit. But this was a gamble for everyone, and good owners were needed who would work for the league's success.

The first to commit was Harry Stavrenos. Harry and I had never been in the same league together, but we had the same baseball "daddy." We both were given our first opportunity in the game by a legendary minor league operator, Marshall Fox. Marshall rarely stayed in the same market for over two or three years and was viewed as a "carny" by some in the game. "Carny" was a pejorative in baseball terminology. It

9. Where in the Hell Is Thunder Bay?

Northern League commissioner and owners, inaugural season. Seated, from left: Bill Pereira, Sioux City; Miles Wolff, commissioner; and Mike Veeck, St. Paul. Second row, from left: Bruce Engel, Duluth; Harry Stavrenos, Sioux Falls; Ricky May, Thunder Bay; Charles Sanders, Rochester; and Marv Goldklang, St. Paul.

referred to a baseball operator who came to town, and like a carnival, stayed just a short time, took as much money from the locals as possible, and then departed in the dead of night. But Marshall knew how to operate and was able to survive in markets where others had failed. Marshall had recommended me to the Atlanta Braves and had hired Harry as an intern right out of college.

Harry ran the San Jose Bees, a team in the California League. For years he was unable to obtain a working agreement with a major league club and was forced to either go the independent route or go out of business. His team became known as the "Bad News" Bees (and occasionally the "Bad Nose" Bees) as he cobbled together a roster of ballplayers rejected by the major leagues. His teams were not always viewed as good citizens, but they were colorful. Major league veterans dotted his lineup, and his 1986 team included 17 players with big-league time. Harry was a passionate owner, running around his park in black Converse All-Star high tops. He seemed a good fit for Sioux Falls. I pushed him to begin lease negotiations with that city.

There's a Bulldozer on Home Plate

Mal Fichman had heard rumors of the effort to start an independent league, and he began calling, wanting to be part of the league. Mal could be controversial, opinionated, and sometimes difficult to work with. Because of this, he often found himself between jobs. But when a team could not obtain a working agreement, they often turned to Mal. Independent teams in Newark, New York; Rocky Mount, North Carolina; Boise, Idaho, and Miami all had been run and managed by Mal. No matter what his detractors said, he was one of the most knowledgeable individuals in baseball, knowing every aspect of the minor leagues both on and off the field. He had also come under the spell of Bob Freitas and believed in the potential of an independent league. Mal did not personally have the money to finance a team, but a businessman on the West Coast was willing to back him. The decision was made to go with Mal and he was steered toward Duluth.

Bill Pereira became interested in Sioux City if the town could build the ballpark. Bill was a highly successful and thoughtful owner of

9. Where in the Hell Is Thunder Bay?

Left and above: Wade Stadium, Duluth, MN. Wade Stadium was built in 1939 and named for the owner of the Duluth Dukes, Frank Wade. It was home for a Northern League team from 1939 to 1942, 1946 to 1970, and 1993 to 2002. It currently is the home for a team in the Northwoods summer collegiate league.

several businesses. He did not initially appear to be the type of owner who would want to be associated with what some were calling an "outlaw league." He owned a profitable affiliated team in Boise, Idaho. However, a few years earlier he needed to run Boise without a major league agreement, and he loved running the team as an independent. He and his son Cord were involved in the high-tech world and his knowledge of the emerging internet would make him a valuable addition to the league if the ballpark could be built in time.

Thunder Bay was a problem. A lease was ready with the city willing to spend funds on improving the facility. However, ownership was nowhere to be found. In the succeeding years in different cities, I found that Canadians were reluctant to take a chance on owning a baseball team. With a hockey club, the situation might have been different, but there was little confidence that baseball could succeed. To find an American owner for a Canadian team was also problematic. Americans believed that doing business in Canada would be different and difficult, and they shied away from baseball investments across the border.

Ricky May, a former Durham Bulls GM, became a prospect for

There's a Bulldozer on Home Plate

Thunder Bay ownership. He had recently sold a sports apparel store and was looking for a new challenge. He was not afraid to take a chance. He did not have enough funds to take on the project by himself, but some of the former Durham Bulls stockholders who had recently done very well on the sale of the Bulls came on board. In truth, some arms may have been twisted, but Ricky ended up with the capitalization he needed. With a heavy Carolina accent and a hard-driving style, Ricky seemed an unusual choice for the reserved Canadian town, but Thunder Bay warmed to him as his excitement on the project transferred to the local fan base.

Marv Goldklang and Mike Veeck were owners the league desperately needed. The pair owned several clubs together, including the Miami Miracle, an independent club in the Florida State League. Marv was also a limited partner in the New York Yankees, and as he liked to say, "Nothing is more limited than being a limited partner with George Steinbrenner." Marv was interested, but he had one condition. He would only own a team if the home city was a direct flight from his home in New Jersey. I wanted to push Marv as a potential owner for Duluth, but not surprisingly, no direct flights existed between Newark and Duluth. Marv had recently been on a rough flight on a regional airline going to see his team in Erie, Pennsylvania. He did not want a repeat. St. Paul was the only city with a direct flight from the Newark, New Jersey, airport. My thought had been that St. Paul would be the most difficult market to find potential ownership. The St. Paul ballpark was only seven miles from the Metrodome, the Minnesota Twins' home. Few in baseball believed that a minor league club in such close proximity to a big-league team could be successful. Now, because of a bumpy flight, a potential owner for that city was in sight.

Mike Veeck, as a partner with Marv, needed to come along on the project, and he was excited. Mike was a great promoter and his presence would cause the media to take notice of the team. Mike was the author of perhaps the greatest promotion in the history of major league baseball. Nearly 100,000 fans showed up. They broke down the gates and spilled onto the field. National attention was huge. And for that, he was blackballed from the game. It was the era of disco music, and Mike, a music fan of almost all styles of music, was not a fan of disco. And thinking that others disliked disco, he staged a promotion where fans would be able to blow up their disco records on the field between games of a doubleheader. It was called "Disco Demolition Night" and the White Sox expected a modest increase in attendance. Management

9. Where in the Hell Is Thunder Bay?

did not realize Mike had struck a nerve, and when a hundred thousand fans tried to get into a park that sat 50,000, bedlam ensued. Between games, the fans rushed the field, blew up the discs, and ruined the field. The second game of the twin bill was canceled and ultimately forfeited because the field was unplayable.

Mike was the son of legendary major league owner Bill Veeck, and he inherited much of his father's showmanship. Bill Veeck owned the Chicago White Sox, Cleveland Indians and St. Louis Browns in his varied career. He was a maverick owner, beloved by fans and hated by fellow owners. His promotions, such as sending a midget to bat in a game, are the stuff of baseball lore. His influence on me was his book *Veeck as in Wreck*, which had been my bible over the years.

It was almost a decade after Disco Demolition before Mike was offered another job in baseball. Marv Goldklang was looking for someone to run his Single-A Florida State League club when Mike's name was mentioned. Pompano Beach was a far cry from the big leagues, but Mike jumped at the opportunity to get back in the game. It worked for both Mike and Marv and when St. Paul came on the horizon, Mike was the right choice to head the operation.

Mike is emotional, funny, creative, and runs a great baseball operation. He has the reputation as a great promoter, which he is, but he is also a nuts-and-bolts baseball man. He understands ticketing, budgets and all the little things that are needed for a franchise to survive. Later, he would go back with big-league clubs on several occasions, but major league baseball was too corporate and buttoned-down for Mike. He always came back to independent ball where he had the freedom to do his thing.

At one point, I told Mike he was really a minor leaguer at heart. He took offense. But it was meant as a compliment. When I referred to people as "big league," it meant that they were bureaucratic, arrogant, and full of themselves. Mike was none of the above. Give me a minor leaguer any time.

The old name of the area's minor league, the Northern League, was the natural name for the league, and it was available. During the spring of 1992 both cities and ownership were getting serious, but still nothing was definite. Getting all the potential groups together to see and meet each other was important. Everyone needed to know that this was real, that other cities and other owners were buying into the dream. A meeting was scheduled in St. Paul to bring city officials and owners together. Municipalities needed to have confidence that other municipalities

There's a Bulldozer on Home Plate

were seriously considering joining the league and were willing to spend money to upgrade the facilities. Owners needed to meet each other and see the quality of the people who were considering ownership. Mayors and recreation directors from eight cities came to the meeting. Possible owners were all present. The meeting went well. Excitement was building on both the city and ownership sides, and both groups expressed a commitment to move forward.

Time was now a factor. The group had been promised that the league would start in June 1993. It was April 1992, but the reality was that only five months were available to have everything set. I needed a final go-ahead from all parties by September. For a franchise to be successful, the preseason is the most important factor in determining success. By September, leases, staff, a business plan, and a dozen other items needed to be in place. Preseason sales of both tickets and sponsorships would be crucial. All the teams would be starting from scratch, and they needed to set up offices. Ballpark renovations would be happening during the fall and winter months, and competent staff needed to be on-site to let the city people know what the priorities were. If everything was not set by September, Sioux City would not start construction on the new ballpark. If things were delayed, it was doubtful that the project could be held together for a 1994 start.

Sioux Falls was the first to commit. In late April, much earlier than expected, the city approved a lease with funds for ballpark improvement. A city councilman, Matt Staab, who was sold on the project, pushed the proposal through. Harry Stavrenos had been on-site much of the spring and his experience gave the city confidence. It was extremely important for the league that this first lease was in hand. Other cities could now point to Sioux Falls as ammunition for their local lease proposals. Duluth was the next to come on board, and then Thunder Bay issued a lease. In late summer, St. Paul finally committed to Marv Goldklang and Mike Veeck. The league was close to being a reality, but everything was not smooth. Sioux City was waiting on Rochester, and the ballclub had no owner.

One potential individual was serious in his intention to own the Rochester team and had been persistent in pushing the league for a franchise. He was the owner of a nearby strip club and bar. I had reservations. On a trip to Rochester, he discussed his potential plans for the team. He wanted to name his club the Black Sox and he was planning to have his dancers as cheerleaders, performing their routines on the dugout roof. I pointed out that the name Black Sox had been given

9. Where in the Hell Is Thunder Bay?

to the Chicago team that had thrown the 1919 World Series and that baseball was really a family sport and perhaps his strippers might not be appropriate. He was not deterred. In checking on his background, a local detective on the Durham police force called the Rochester police department to quietly obtain some information on the individual. The Rochester police force refused to even acknowledge that they ever had heard of the man, despite newspaper reports indicating that the nightclub and its owner were well known to local constabulary. I decided to pass on him as a potential member of the Northern League. (Within six months he would sue the league for his exclusion, but the suit, although costly, was thrown out. The following year he started his own league, the Great Central League, which barely lasted one season.)

Finally, with no other choices, it became necessary for me to fund the Rochester team. As I faced a potential conflict-of-interest problem if I was both commissioner and owner, Charles Sanders, the former CFO of the Atlanta Braves, was convinced to become the president and operator of the Rochester team. I would provide the capital, but he would run the team as if it were his own. Charles had been in charge of the minor league business operations of the Braves' farm teams and was very knowledgeable. His professional baseball background gave the league's ownership roster another solid addition.

The Northern League now had five cities. It was time for the mayor of Sioux City to step up and make good on his promise of a new ballpark. I was present at a city council meeting in Sioux City in late September 1992 that would decide the fate of the ballpark and the league. It was a tense time. Community opposition had surfaced, and the council chambers were full of those opposed to a new ballpark. One of the opponents was the former play-by-play announcer of the Sioux City Soos of the Three-I League, the last minor league team in that city, a club that folded after the 1960 season. He had seen baseball fail in Sioux City, and he argued heatedly that it would happen again. I had been in these situations before, and it was always impossible to predict how the politicians would vote when controversy surfaced. Fortunately, the mayor was strong—he had the votes—and the funds were appropriated for a new ballpark. Sioux City was now the sixth team in the new Northern League. The league was officially in business.

10

Who Would Want to Play Independent Ball?

One of the questions always asked was, "How are you going to get players?" Minor league baseball is accustomed to having players supplied by the major league affiliate. Finding talent, spring training, scouting, tryout camps and a dozen other worries were not something affiliated minor league teams had to worry about. The few minor league teams that had to operate independently had seen mixed success. The 1980 Rocky Mount (N.C.) Pines of the Carolina League ended with an abysmal 24 wins and 114 losses while the 1987 Salt Lake City Trappers won a record 29 straight games and the pennant in the Pioneer League. The Northern League needed to fill a whole league. Was the talent available? Would the product be any good?

My answer was always "yes," although in truth, I had little on which to base any answer. I would point out that each year Major League Baseball drafted around 1,500 new players. That meant that 1,500 players would be pushed out of the farm systems to make room for the new talent. Many of these players were not ready to retire and might be available. Most important, these were quality players that MLB signed and trained for three or four years. Some received significant bonuses. Bob Freitas had always preached the need for a "second chance" league, and the Northern League could fill that void. Also, a large pool of graduating college seniors would be available. College baseball had become a much-improved product over the previous 20 years, and many good college players were never drafted.

The ability to obtain players was enhanced by the fact that many of our owners had already operated independently and had successfully found players for their teams. Van Schley was one of the most important owners in this regard. He was part of the St. Paul ownership group, and for the previous dozen years, he had supplied players for independent teams. He caught the baseball bug after reading an article in *Sports*

10. Who Would Want to Play Independent Ball?

Illustrated in 1977 about an independent team operating in the short-lived Lone Star League whose players were sleeping on the beach because of missing paychecks. He called that Texas City team and began supplying and paying players. Van had no baseball background, but he hired experienced and quality baseball men as managers, and together they put solid teams on the field. In the succeeding years he would be involved with Grays Harbor, Washington; Victoria, British Columbia; and Utica, New York. He finally hit the national scene with his remarkable Salt Lake City Trappers.

Bob Freitas introduced me to Van, and I was with him and saw his joy when he sold his first player to a major league organization. We became friends. When I started the Durham Bulls, he was one of the few willing to take a chance on the dream. When he needed help in Utica, I set up the front office and developed the business side for him. At the Winter Meetings, he was the first person to seek out. His sense of fun was huge, and he seemed to know every great restaurant and bar in North America. His wife called him the "concierge to the world." His contact list was immense, and he brought Bill Murray, Jimmy Buffett and others into the independent teams as investors. When I started the quest for the Northern League, his success with independent teams gave credibility to my push for investors. Van's interest was not the business end of baseball but the players, and he was truly skilled at finding players and convincing them to come to independent baseball. The teams he worked with were always winners.

Van brought Nick Belmonte on board early in the formation of the Northern League. Nick became the director of player personnel for the entire league. Nick was a former minor league player and had also managed Salt Lake City for Van. He had outstanding contacts, and his role with the league was to backstop clubs if they were having difficulty finding a player. We found out quickly that finding players was not going to be as difficult as some had speculated. That first year Nick had two tryout camps in Florida and Texas, and nearly 300 players showed up. Most could play. Resumes and phone calls from players inundated the various offices.

Early speculation was that the league might be the equivalent of a low Single-A or rookie league with young players predominating, but over that first winter, experienced players, including ex-big leaguers, made contact, looking for a place to play. Prior to the Northern League, if a player was released by a major league organization, he had very few options. He might go to Mexico or Japan, but those leagues had limits of

There's a Bulldozer on Home Plate

two or three foreign players. Effectively, a player's career was over when he received a pink slip from a big-league organization.

However, many players still wanted to play, still had the dream alive, and the Northern League became a good option. In the early spring of 1993, I was in the office at *Baseball America* when a call was forwarded to me. A former player for the Twins, Phillies and White Sox, Jeff Bittiger, was on the line, wanting to know about playing in the league. I knew of Jeff when he had been one of the top prospects in the Carolina League. He questioned me about league managers. He knew the Rochester skipper and asked for the phone number. Jeff signed a contract and became one of the top pitchers and then one of the top pitching coaches in the league over the next decade. He would twice be sold to major league organizations, but he always came back to the league.

The same experience happened as teams searched for field managers. Would a respected and experienced minor league manager be willing to come to a start-up league? At the winter meetings, prior to the first season, I ran into "Singin' Ed" Nottle, a longtime minor league player and manager. The nickname had come when he released an album of his singing standards while backed by the Oakland Symphony Orchestra. Ed had spent several seasons as the Boston Red Sox Triple-A manager, and it had been rumored that he was seriously considered for the manager position with the big-league club. But he had been let go instead and was looking for a managing job at the meetings. I asked him if he would come to a new league, never expecting him to consider the position. Without hesitation, he said yes. I quickly put him in touch with Sioux City ownership, and for the next 15 years, Ed managed in independent ball.

The other clubs found quality managers. Frank Verdi, a longtime Triple-A manager, went to Sioux Falls, and former big-league catcher and minor league manager Tim Blackwell was hired by St. Paul. Salt Lake City coach Dan Shwam was hired by Thunder Bay, and Mal Fichman named himself manager in Duluth. Rochester struggled in its search, with owner Charles Sanders being hounded for the job by a journeyman minor league catcher, Doug Simunic. Simunic would call almost every day, and finally, worn down by the calls, Sanders hired Simunic. For the next 25 years, Simunic was one of the leading managers in independent baseball, winning over 1,300 games.

Over the winter months, things moved quickly. Front offices were in place, sponsorship sales were surprisingly good, ballpark improvements

10. Who Would Want to Play Independent Ball?

Northern League Organizational meeting. This photograph was taken in the fall of 1992 in St. Paul, Minn., as owners and staff met for the first time together to set up policies and rules for the new league. Seated, from left: Tom Leip, executive director; Miles Wolff, commissioner; and Mike Veeck, St. Paul co-owner. Back row, from left: Tom Van Schaack, Duluth GM; Bruce Engel, Duluth owner; Nick Belmonte, director of player procurement; Harry Stavrenos, Sioux Falls owner; Ricky May, Thunder Bay owner; Charles Sanders, Rochester owner; Van Schley, St. Paul; Marv Goldklang, St. Paul; Bill Pereira, Sioux City; and David Kemp, league historian.

were moving forward, and player contracts were being signed. The league office needed someone on-site to handle the operations in the area. I hired Tom Leip, an excellent GM from the Northwest League, to be the executive director of the league. He moved to the Twin Cities and set up an office in his home. He handled all player contracts, started league-wide marketing, and oversaw hiring a crew of umpires to officiate league games.

So many concerns were involved with the opening of a new team, and now we were opening a new league. The truth was that no one knew if anyone would show up on Opening Day. There were no season tickets to renew, no longtime base of fans. Would the weather cooperate? The opener was in many ways the harbinger of the rest of the season. If the fans didn't come out, we were doomed.

There's a Bulldozer on Home Plate

One concern had been the Sioux City ballpark. Would the facility be completed in the eight-month building time frame? The weather that spring had not been good. Fortunately, everything was on time on the construction schedule, and the ballpark was completed before the June opener. In the rest of the league, the weather was beautiful for the June 15 openers. Crowds packed the stadiums on Opening Day, and enthusiasm for the league was strong. For some cities, it had been 20 years since there had been a professional game, and the thrill of having a team was evident. Observers called it a "celebration of summer" in an area of the country that had seen a harsh winter and a wet spring. The Northern League became a national story, and publications such as *Sports Illustrated* wrote feature articles on the league.

There were those who dismissed the league. Andy McPhail, GM of the Minnesota Twins, was reported to have called the league a "beer league," and a few of the Twin Cities baseball writers wrote that it was nothing more than "town ball." But the quality of baseball was much better than most had expected, and the fans were not deterred by the few naysayers.

St. Paul was the poster child for the league, and its success carried over to other league cities. When Mike Veeck had committed to the franchise, he believed he might be able to average 2,000 to 3,000 fans a game. Soon he had to readjust that estimate as every game became a sellout. A Saints ticket was the hottest ticket in the Twin Cities. The concern had always been the Minnesota Twins, but that proved to be the Saints' biggest selling point. The Twins played in the Metrodome, a monstrous, concrete indoor facility. Unbeknownst to Veeck and others, fans wanted to go outside to see a baseball game, not indoors to the Metrodome. Some fans were delightedly waiting for a rainout. A writer for the *Wall Street Journal*, Stefan Fatsis, came and wrote a book on the league, *Wild and Outside*, the title mirroring the spirit of the Saints' Midway Stadium.

As word spread on the quality of the league, more big-league veterans started appearing on rosters. Former Los Angeles Dodger Pedro Guerrero, a five-time National League all-star and World Series MVP, signed with Sioux Falls. Leon "Bull" Durham, a Chicago Cub great, became a St. Paul Saint. All told, twelve former major leaguers played in the league in 1993 with every team having at least one big-league player. Major League scouts were showing up at games, and players were sold during the season. Kash Beauchamp, a former first-round draft pick, was sold to the Cincinnati Reds. He was hitting .367 for Rochester when

10. Who Would Want to Play Independent Ball?

Sioux City, Iowa. Lewis and Clark Park was completed in just eight months over the winter and spring of 1992–93. Its construction enabled the first of the independent leagues, the Northern League, to complete its membership and operate that first season. The city's old ballpark, home of the Sioux City Soos, had been torn down, but the confidence of the city fathers that baseball would succeed in their city gave birth to the new facility.

he was sold and then hit .400 after reporting to Double-A Chattanooga. Other players from that first season made the jump to affiliated baseball, and five would ultimately appear on big-league rosters.

It was important that the players who went to major league organizations were sold. Major League Baseball recognized Northern League contracts. Players could not arbitrarily leave a Northern League roster if a big-league club was interested in their services. With contracts recognized by MLB's office in New York, credibility grew for the league. The sale price for a player was set at $3,000, which often did not cover a team's investment in the player. Each club paid a player his salary and his transportation to come to the league. With a sale, the team then had additional costs of finding and bringing in a replacement player. But with recognition by MLB, a precedent was set for the Northern League and the other independent leagues that followed.

The year was phenomenal. There were glitches along the way, but no one noticed. Every team, except Rochester, made money. St. Paul had sellouts for most games, and Thunder Bay, one of the question marks

There's a Bulldozer on Home Plate

St. Paul, Minnesota. St. Paul's Midway Stadium was one of the huge successes in independent baseball. From 1993 to 2014, almost every game of the St. Paul Saints was a sellout. In 2015, the team moved to a new downtown stadium and continued its amazing success. The original Midway Stadium had been built as a home for the Saints of the Triple A American Association. But when major league baseball came to the Twin Cities in 1961, the Saints moved and Midway Stadium was torn down. However, the city of St. Paul built a new Midway Stadium to host amateur teams, and when the Northern League was formed as the first of the new independent leagues, Midway Stadium was again home of the Saints.

at the start, was second in attendance, averaging almost 4,000 a game. Ricky May selected the team colors, teal and purple, not traditional baseball hues. Ricky had been in the sports apparel business and knew these were the current hot colors for apparel. I attended the final game of the season in Thunder Bay, bringing Mr. Mount and my son Hoffman on the trip. Mr. Mount had been such a help over the years, and I wanted him to see what had been created. Hoffman had followed the new league with a nine-year-old's excitement and it was a treat for him. We sat in the bleachers and were amazed that the entire ballpark was a sea of teal. Everyone in the stands was wearing a Whiskey Jacks teal hat. It was impressive.

After that game I entered the Thunder Bay clubhouse to

10. Who Would Want to Play Independent Ball?

congratulate manager Dan Shwam on a good season. I asked him a question that had been on my mind most of the season: "How many of your players will want to come back next season?" I expected him to say three or four. One of the hopes in forming the league had been that there would be some continuity in players from season to season. Many minor league clubs had a new roster every season, and it was often difficult to build allegiance for an affiliated team. I hoped the Northern League would be different.

Dan looked up at me. "If I went around the clubhouse right now and asked each player, all 22 would ask to come back." I stared at him in wonder, and he explained. "This is baseball like they've always dreamed since they were little boys. The politics of a farm system aren't part of the scene here. In a major league organization, the players that signed for the most money are the ones who play. Here, they don't have to worry about who is doing what in the league above or below them. If they play well, they will stay in the lineup. They are playing to win, not to pad their statistics. With a roster limit of 22 players, everyone has a role. And they are heroes in Thunder Bay. It may not be the big leagues, but for most of them, this will be their big leagues."

11

"Let's Start Our Own League"

Baseball prior to the start of the Northern League had been a closed industry. It had become a monopoly, and no new leagues or teams were welcomed. Over the prior decade, a few new proposed leagues had attempted to join the National Association, the controlling organization of minor league baseball. All were turned down. The major leagues had limited the number of farm clubs, and the only option for a city that was without a team was to try to convince an existing team to move. But many markets were outside the geographical range of the 16 minor leagues, with little hope that they could ever obtain a team. With this scarcity, the values of minor league teams soared, and whereas earlier minor league teams could be bought for debts, now the values were in the millions.

It never occurred to these cities that they did not need the National Association. Then the Northern League happened, eyes were opened, and dreams unleashed. Over the next four years, twelve new leagues were formed that called themselves independent. No standards, entry fees, or requirements were needed, and cities were giving leases to people with few credentials. Most of these leagues were formed by individuals who had no experience in running a team, and many were in cities that did not have the population base to support a club. But hope springs eternal in the human breast, and everyone believed it was easy to start a baseball league. The fans would certainly show up. "If you build it, they will come," was the belief. The reality was different.

That 1993 season had seen another independent league, the Frontier League, start. League membership was made up of small cities in West Virginia, Kentucky, and Ohio and was formed by a former Appalachian League general manager, Bud Bickel. The league began play on June 30, and on July 12, two teams, Wayne, West Virginia, and Ashland, Kentucky, folded. Other markets such as Paintsville, Kentucky, and Lancaster, Ohio, were just too small to support any type of professional baseball, and it appeared that the league would not operate

11. "Let's Start Our Own League"

a second season. But league directors saw what was happening in the Northern League and saw that independent baseball could work. They hired an experienced minor league executive, Bill Lee (not the former Red Sox pitcher), who had successfully operated both professional baseball and hockey teams. Lee began making approaches to larger cities for league membership. He gave direction to individual teams on operational procedures, and the Frontier League became a stable independent league that survived.

In 1994 the Texas-Louisiana League began play, and it appeared to have a good chance for success. It was started by Dallas businessman Byron Pierce and former U.S. Congressman John Bryant. For three years, they had been trying to join the minor league organization but had been rebuffed. The group had actually tried to steal all the affiliated Appalachian League agreements and have them move to Texas. They were unsuccessful. The pair had good markets whose minor league ballparks were still standing. The Northern League gave them confidence to operate without the minor league blessing, and the first year was good. Cities like Amarillo, Mobile and Corpus Christi were hungry for baseball, and the quality was good. It was a requirement to have former big leaguers as managers, and that helped the league with credibility. The Texas-Louisiana League would survive.

The outlook wasn't brilliant for the other two other leagues that started in 1994. Both were started by men who had been rejected by the Northern League. The North Central League was organized by a Minnesota pharmacist who had hoped to run the Duluth franchise. He envisioned a Duluth team stocked almost entirely by players from his home state. Minnesota was not a center for baseball talent, and the league cautioned him that this would not work. The druggist insisted, and the league moved on to other potential owners.

The pharmacist persisted, and in 1994 he formed the North Central League. Early league directives for 15 area players on each roster were canceled when managers could not find the players. The requirement was dropped to four. He had hoped that smaller Minnesota cities such as Austin, Mankato and St. Cloud might join, but these cities fell through. When the league started, it had six cities stretching from Brainerd, Minnesota, to Saskatoon, Saskatchewan, a 17-hour bus ride. Ownership was difficult to find, and the league had to take over the Marshall (Minn.) Mallards one day before the season started when the original owner disclosed he had no equipment, insurance or meal money. The Mallards were locked out of the ballpark on August 2 due to non-payment of rent, and the league limped to the end of the season.

The North Central might be considered a bright spot if it were compared to the Great Central League. The Great Central gave the word "disaster" new meaning:

Great Central League
The History of Independent Baseball Leagues 1993–2002,
Miles Wolff and David Kemp

If ever there was an independent league that demonstrated everything that could go wrong in a start-up league, it was the Great Central. The league was thrown together with little planning or time. It was organized by a Minnesota modular home dealer and strip club owner who had attempted to gain entry into the Northern League in 1993. He was turned down and then decided to create his own league.

He had hoped to start with six cities, but only four were ready, Lafayette, Ind.; Champaign-Urbana, Ill.; Mason City, Iowa; and Minneapolis. The facility at Champaign-Urbana had no lights. Parade Field in Minneapolis, a recreation facility, had no rest rooms (unless one counts the area often used by players behind the left field light pole). Spring training for the Lafayette Leopards started two weeks before the June 14 opener. The other three franchises held no practices until three days before the start of the season, partly because their GMs had not been hired until early June.

A few highlights can be mentioned. Opening Day in Lafayette drew the largest crowd of the season, 1,294, and in July, two players were sold to major league organizations. The lowlights are more plentiful. No hotels were scheduled for some road trips, and one charter bus was not large enough to handle the 20-man roster and team equipment. Debts were everywhere. One fan paid an $800 laundry bill so that the Lafayette team could get its uniforms and play a weekend series. In Minneapolis, the 70-year-old mother of a league official who disagreed with a scoring decision reportedly punched out the official scorer. On July 27, the Lafayette GM and his staff quit. The GM had not received a paycheck since arriving on April 18. On August 14 the entire Mason City Bats team quit. Rather than disband the franchise, the league found replacements and the new team went 0–15, losing one three-game series by a combined score of 65–10. The Champaign-Urbana Bandits went through six managers in 67 games.

The entire Minneapolis Millers team refused to play on August 2 because of its dislike for manager George Scott, the former Boston Red Sox great. Scott was fired, then rehired as GM. A busload of handicapped children coming to a scheduled Millers game was never informed that the game had been canceled. Millers players living in the Augsburg College dorm were thrown out of the dorm after an alleged gang rape of a 17-year-old student. The Millers

11. "Let's Start Our Own League"

then sued the college for improper ejection from the dorm. A Christian radio station broadcasting the games canceled its contract with the team shortly thereafter. On August 26 seven players for Lafayette left the team, having not been paid in August. Playoffs were canceled. No final statistics were published because the league statistician had never been paid. The attendance leader in the league was Lafayette, drawing 11,682 for the season, an average crowd of 365 per game. The league did not operate in the following season.

The examples of the North Central and Great Central in 1994 neither warned nor deterred other leagues from giving independent baseball a try, and in 1995, eleven leagues started the season. The Golden State League started, played 10 games, and folded. One city, Rosamond, California, started but did not make it through Opening Day. In the fifth inning, the city refused to turn on the lights because ownership had not paid the deposit for the field. The Atlantic Coast League lasted a bit longer, 17 games, until player payroll was due and funds were not available. In the North Atlantic League, the Massachusetts (Lynn) Mad Dogs made a road trip to Nashua in August only to find out that the Nashua players had left the team after not being paid. The league refused to admit the team had folded and for the remaining Nashua games the league announced that each game had been rained out.

Decorum and civility were not always in evidence. In the Texas-Louisiana League, a manager punched out his team's GM when he refused to give enough baseballs for batting practice. In Tyler, Texas, a player's wife started fighting a female front-office employee over her husband's paycheck. In Abilene, Texas, a bench-clearing brawl included the team mascot, Davey Crockett. Davey was ejected from the game. This was not the only mascot with problems. In Bend, Oregon, Rowdy the Raccoon was arrested for menacing when the mascot saw a former girlfriend and her child in the stands and started pelting them with rocks. A few days earlier, the PA announcer had been ejected from the press box when he began reading the announcement for LensCrafters Eye Center during an argument between the home team's manager and the umpires.

In the Western League, an owner chased the umpires off the field in a dispute over ball-strike calls. In the Northeast League, the commissioner took over the umpiring chores in one game when the scheduled umpires failed to show. The Sioux Falls Canaries saw the owner rush on the field to dispute a fair-foul home run call on a round-tripper by St. Paul's Leon "Bull" Durham. The umpires, unaware that this was the owner, had the police eject him from the stadium. The league then suspended the owner for the remainder of the season. Former big leaguer Kevin Mitchell was suspended for nine games when he slugged his owner when the owner came onto the field during a brawl.

Independent clubs had the ability to buy and sell players, but some transactions were unusual. In the Texas-Louisiana League, the Greenville Bluesmen traded for a pitcher in exchange for a case of baseballs and ten pounds of Mississippi catfish. In the Big South League, a player was traded for cash and a Muddy Waters album. And future major leaguer Kerry Ligtenberg was sold to the Atlanta Braves for six dozen baseballs and two dozen bats.

Promotions were different and more outrageous in the independent leagues. Palm Springs tried a Come-to-the-Ballpark-Naked-Night but community pressure forced a cancellation of the event. The team was able to hold a Transvestite Night. St. Paul held a Viagra Inflatable Bat night. Unique names occasionally showed up on lineup cards. Former Negro League star Ted "Double Duty" Radcliffe made an appearance for Schaumburg, while Olympic skier Bode Miller played outfield for the Nashua Pride. With new teams and new leagues everywhere, new situations developed that were not part of the normal baseball experience. It was not always easy for the league office.

conversation between the league president and league commissioner

"We just had a complaint on the pig in St. Paul."
"Oh, no. What's the complaint?"
"The Duluth manager has called to say the pig that takes the baseballs to the umpires defecated on home plate in the 6th inning."
"He actually used the word 'defecate'?"
"Absolutely. What do you want to do?"
"I'm not sure the bowel movements of a pig are the commissioner's concern. OK. Tell him that I will call the St. Paul GM and issue a stern warning that it is against league rules for animals to take a dump on home plate in the course of play. If it happens again, the pig will either be fined or barbequed. Will that take care of it?"
"It should."
"Amazing. I don't think I've ever heard anyone in baseball say 'defecate.'"

12

Growth

While other leagues struggled, the Northern League continued to prosper. In 1994 Sam Katz, seeing the league's successful first year, brought Winnipeg into the league. He purchased the Rochester Aces franchise for less than $200,000, which almost covered Rochester's debts. I had hoped that a sale would cover all loans. But the league needed Winnipeg—it would be the largest city in the league—and it would not be possible to fund the Aces for another season. Sam knew this. The deal was done.

Winnipeg had no baseball facility and the team would have to play in the stadium of the Winnipeg Blue Bombers of the Canadian Football League. The facility could seat over 20,000 fans and was barely adequate for baseball. Home plate was in a corner of the end zone with few seats, and the left field foul line was generously listed at 260 feet with a 40-foot-high wire fence. The press box was at the top of the upper deck, probably 300 feet from the batter's box. The playing surface was a bouncy artificial turf. But with all the inadequacies, it worked. It was a unique and funky place to watch a baseball game, and the fans loved it.

Sam Katz was a successful businessman in Winnipeg, which included being a promoter of rock and roll shows. For several years prior, he had tried to bring Triple-A baseball to Winnipeg. He was turned down chiefly because of travel concerns with the city being too distant from the Triple-A leagues. One year, he brought the Toronto Blue Jays to town for an exhibition game, but his only hope for professional baseball in his city became the Northern League. He became one of the strong owners in the league, and due in some measure to his success as owner, he became mayor of Winnipeg and served for two four-year terms.

For the first three years, the Northern League was a six-team league. The first season the league played a 72-game season, and by 1995, the schedule was up to 84 games. As commissioner, I was trying to add new markets, and by 1996, two cities were ready for entry: Fargo, North Dakota, and Madison, Wisconsin. The Fargo club was officially named

There's a Bulldozer on Home Plate

the Fargo-Moorhead RedHawks, which included the name of Moorhead, Minnesota, a city of some 35,000 souls which bordered Fargo across the Red River. Madison would become the Madison Black Wolf. It was a city that a decade earlier had enjoyed huge success in the affiliated Midwest League.

Fargo had been one of the prime targets for membership when the Northern League was formed in 1993. However, the baseball facility was controlled by the American Legion and the league was unable to reach arrangements with the Legion for dual use of the ballpark. Our efforts stirred interest in the city, and a movement was started to build a new baseball facility in the town. The most important supporter of a new ballpark was North Dakota State University, which needed a ballpark for its collegiate baseball program. As momentum gained for the ballpark, several local groups started vying for ownership of the franchise. It became contentious, but ultimately the ownership was headed by Otter Tail Power Company, the largest public utility in the state of North Dakota. For the league, this was a huge image builder. The ties to the state university and the public utility gave the league the appearance of stability and success.

The ballpark was to be built on the NDSU campus over the fall and winter of 1995. Winters in Fargo give enhanced definition to the word "frigid," and the question for the league was whether the stadium would be ready for Opening Day. Fortunately, one of the top executives of Otter Tail Power, Bruce Thom, was taking a personal interest in the project. He became president of the ballclub and was a major influence in the construction project. Even with push from both the ballclub and the university, the facility was not totally finished by Opening Day 1996. This time, however, the American Legion let the team use its ballpark, and the first series was played in that park. Two weeks later, I was called upon to give approval for the new ballpark. The sod for the field had only been put down a few days prior to the newly scheduled opening. Normally, two weeks were needed for sod to knit into the dirt of the playing field. I walked on the field with officials and media waiting anxiously as I tested the grass. In truth, I had no expertise in this area. Although the field felt soft and squishy, I was not about to tell the team's players that they could not play in the new ballpark. I ruled that everything was perfect. The game was played that night in a gorgeous new brick ballpark with a packed house. No player broke his leg on the loose sod, and I was now an expert on laying sod.

Madison was a different story. The ballpark was ready, and although

12. Growth

Winnipeg, Manitoba. To accommodate the arrival of the Northern League in 1994, Winnipeg Stadium, home of the Winnipeg Blue Bombers of the Canadian Football League, was reconfigured in order to have baseball played in the park. The artificial turf facility had home plate deep in the end zone with the left field corner only 260 feet from home plate. It was different, but it worked. The photograph shows a night when a crowd of more than 20,000 was in attendance.

it was modest at best, it had housed an affiliated team just two years earlier. The potential looked good for the league. The population base was excellent, and a competent front office was in place. But the city had been burnt by previous ownerships, and there was no push by city fathers to get a new team. I was the push to bring baseball to the city. Making several trips to the market, I arranged a lease and found local ownership. The league needed the eighth city to pair with Fargo. Excitement was minimal, and the franchise languished. Excellent teams were supplied, but the franchise never clicked.

Sometimes, it is difficult to explain why a team fails in a city. Madison was one of those cities. It had all the elements that an operator looks for in a market, but it simply didn't work. The lawyer who bought the franchise was undercapitalized, and with disappointing attendance numbers, he ultimately turned the franchise back to the league. As happened with the Rochester Aces and later with the Duluth-Superior

There's a Bulldozer on Home Plate

Dukes, I took over the team and supplied the capital, hoping new ownership could be found. Finally, a group from Lincoln, Nebraska, applied to become a member of the league and a sale was completed. I was able to recoup my loans. Lincoln came in with strong ownership and a new $30-million facility and we departed Madison.

The Madison Black Wolf lasted five years in the league. As the Madison operation struggled, local pundits argued that Madison, with a strong University of Wisconsin football program, was a football town, not a baseball town. That is why the team was failing, they said. That excuse might have worked, except immediately after the Northern League left, a summer college team took over the lease and became the most profitable franchise in all of summer college baseball, averaging nearly 5,000 a game. This contrasted with the Black Wolf, a professional franchise that averaged fewer than 2,000 fans per game. My view of the market proved correct—it did have the elements for a successful operation—but the key to open the city's potential was never found by the Northern League. Other teams in the Northern League would fail over the years, but Madison remained one of the most frustrating to look back on.

The memories of Madison weren't bad. With the state capital and the university, it was always a vibrant community to visit. Two of the Black Wolf players became instrumental in the entry into the Quebec City market. Ila Borders was a member of the team for a season and demonstrated that a woman could pitch in a professional league. "Dirty Al" Gallagher came in to manage. It was the last time I would have Al manage one of my teams. The memories of Al are always good.

"Dirty Al" Gallagher

His parents could not decide on a name for their son, and so they named him all the names they had considered. His full name was Alan Mitchell Edward George Patrick Henry Gallagher. These are certainly all fine names, but parental pride was probably somewhat muted when the name that stuck was "Dirty Al." The name fit, and the stories are varied on how his sobriquet was earned. The most frequently recounted tale involves his college years when his team was on a win streak and he vowed not to shower or wash his uniform and sweat gear until the team lost a game. A 46-game win streak helped earn Al the well-deserved name. Even if this tale were fiction, the name would undoubtedly have been bestowed at some point in his career. Showers were not high on his to-do list, and his uniform, with tobacco juice drippings, often seemed to have avoided the daily clubhouse washes.

Dirty Al spent four years in the major leagues as a third baseman until

12. Growth

injuries cut his big-league career short. Most of his big-league career was spent with his hometown San Francisco Giants, and his minor league career lasted 13 seasons. After playing, he spent 25 years as a minor league manager, 16 of them in the independent leagues. For ten years before the advent of the independent leagues, he was out of the game, and during that time he was a sixth-grade schoolteacher. I always had trouble envisioning Al as an elementary teacher. Al could be profane and outrageous on the field, but then I can only imagine that this would endear Al to his students as opposed to school administrators.

Many factors went into the success of the Durham Bulls, but Al Gallagher had to be one of the most important. Many minor league managers are colorless and view the job as developing the prospects on the team with no indication that winning matters. Dealing with the press is just a distasteful obligation of the job. Al viewed winning as totally important, and he loved interacting with writers. In that first season in Durham, Al turned on both the fans and the media to the joy of minor league baseball. He was flamboyant on the field and would spend hours with the press. In the Bulls' first-ever televised game, he was ejected, then put on a show and finally deposited a wad of chewing tobacco on home plate. He won and also developed players. The 1980 club was 84–56 with ten members of that team making the big leagues. A typical minor league manager may never have provided the spark that ignited Durham's love for the Bulls.

Another member of that 1980 team never made the big leagues but later in his career was named "Best Western Poet in the United States." Paul "Red" Shuttleworth was a boyhood friend of Al. Red came to visit Al in Durham during the summer of 1980 and ended up staying most of the season with the team. He would dress with the team, sit on the bench with Al and occasionally take the role of bullpen catcher. His other role was to drink with Al and coach Leo Mazzone after the games. We would joke that we were the only club in professional baseball with a "team poet." Several of his poems on that 1980 season were published.

"Dirty Al" Gallagher stories are nearly as numerous as those of his mentor, "Scrap Iron" Courtney. One of the best recounts a brawl between the hated rivals, the Los Angeles Dodgers and the San Francisco Giants. Both teams were in a full-scale melee as a voice could be heard amidst the clamor. The voice kept repeating "get Fox, get Fox," as the fight escalated. Charlie Fox was the San Francisco manager. When everything was over and things were being sorted out, the question arose as to who had been yelling to get the Giants manager. It had not been a Dodger. It was the Giant third baseman, Al Gallagher, who hated his skipper.

If one did not know Al and looked at his career, the view would be that he must be a grizzled old-school veteran who had trouble relating to younger players. But Al always was a player's manager, and he seemed to get along with everyone except umpires. Even when he was in his sixties, still managing, his spirit was youthful. In 1999 Ila Borders came to pitch for the Madison Black Wolf in the Northern League. Ila was one of the first females ever to play professional baseball, and many of the traditionalists were outraged that she had been signed to a contract. They viewed her as purely a publicity stunt, pushed by the front office in hopes of drawing a few more fans. Ila did not view herself as any sort of stunt. She was deadly serious about pitching, and Al welcomed her. In her book, Making My Pitch, Ila says of Al, "It was an honor to play for him. He was one of the best managers I played for, easygoing and supportive."

Al understood Ila's strengths and weaknesses, and he used them well. She was lefthanded which was a plus. She did not throw hard, upper 70s, but she had a good breaking pitch and good control. Al made a starter out of Ila. She had been used almost exclusively in the bullpen in the prior two seasons, many times in mop-up roles. By making her a starter, the media would take notice and the start would be publicized. Most important, the opposing team would have time to get psyched up. Al understood that players' egos would get in the way. No batter wanted to be "struck out by a girl." A player would see that slow curve coming toward the plate and would over-swing. After three or so innings, Al would take Ila out of the game. The opposing lineup had seen Ila and could adjust to her velocity. At that point, Al would bring in a hard-throwing righthander, and the opposing team had to make another adjustment. It worked. Ila finished the season with the best ERA on the team, 1.67, and her record was 1–0 in 12 starts and 32 innings pitched.

In his early years, Al was hard-driving and intense. His first marriage ended in divorce. But he stopped drinking, remarried, and mellowed. In 2012, at age 66, he was both field manager and general manager in McAllen, Texas. The league was floundering, about to go under, but Al kept his team together. The team ended in last place, the league folded, and it was Al's last year in baseball. He retired to the West Coast and died in 2018. Al Gallagher was unique and special, and to repeat Ila Borders, it was an honor to work with him.

The Northern League continued to evolve and by 2000, only one of the original ownership groups was still in place. The St. Paul Saints with Mike Veeck and Marv Goldklang remained stable. Other owners saw the value of their franchises rise, and they cashed out. Duluth was the first to sell, and the sale took place after the first season. The Duluth owner, seeing the success of the Northern League, started his own league on the west coast, the Western League. His sale price was a reported $500,000. Thunder Bay was next and it sold for around $750,000. In 1998 the franchise moved to a new stadium and bigger market in Schaumburg, Illinois. Harry Stavrenos, the first owner to commit to the league, sold in

12. Growth

1998 for a reported $1.5 million. Sioux City was sold to manager Ed Nottle, who convinced a group of local investors to purchase the club from the Pereira family. The estimated sale price was over $1 million. All the initial owners had taken a chance on independent baseball, and the initial $50,000 fee turned into a solid investment.

For myself, as organizer of the league, I was gratified to see the league growing in value, but it was a bit sad to see the first group of owners leave. These owners believed in the dream and made it happen. New owners were not always as knowledgeable, and from a commissioner's point of view, their inexperience made running the league more difficult. The new owners paid a good price for membership in the league but often expected more than was possible from minor league sports.

Photograph taken at the 2019 American Association All-Star Game in St. Paul, Minn. Along with Miles and Michelle Wolff are Darryl Strawberry and Ila Borders, former St. Paul players.

At times I would remark that owning a baseball team kills brain cells. I would see bright and successful businessmen and lawyers do really dumb things when it came to owning a team. I could rationalize lawyers making awful business decisions, because their only product was the hours they charge their clients. Lawyers never had to implement their own advice. But businessmen should have understood that the purpose of a business was to make money. Yet these groups become so enamored of their teams that they would spend silly money on the players when they should have been paying attention to the bottom line.

There's a Bulldozer on Home Plate

League meetings took hours as owners bickered over getting one more Saturday home date in the schedule when more pressing matters were ignored. Late-night phone calls were frequent from disgruntled owners.

conversation between league president and league commissioner

"I had a phone call last night from the Winnipeg Goldeyes' owner. He's not a happy camper."

"What's the problem?"

"He's accusing one of the St. Paul players of trying to kill his mascot, Goldie."

"This is for real?"

"Yes. Goldie was jumping up and down on the top of the St. Paul dugout, and it was bothering one of their players. The player jumped out of the dugout, pulled the mascot on the field, and according to Winnipeg observers, he was trying to choke the mascot with a broom handle over his throat. I talked to the St. Paul manager, and he swears there was no intent to kill the mascot."

"What do the umpires say?"

"They do agree that the mascot was annoying, and they did throw the player out of the game. However, they won't comment on whether physical harm was intended by the player."

"All right, let's suspend the player for a couple of games and make it league policy that players can't abuse mascots. And let's tell the Goldeyes to tone down Goldie."

I was becoming more involved in other aspects of independent baseball and in 1999 was named commissioner of the Northeast League. That league started in 1995 and seemed doomed to failure, but somehow it had hung on. Better markets were looking to join the league, and I had an interest in purchasing a franchise in the league. When the opportunity arose to become commissioner, I accepted the position. I remained head of the Northern League and for four seasons the two leagues operated as one, with a Northern League Central division (the original league) and the Northern League East division (the Northeast League). There was no interleague play, but at the conclusion of each season, the champions of each division played for the title.

In late 1998 my family and I moved to Quebec City to start a team. With a new league and a new team, it was time to make some decisions.

12. Growth

For 19 years I was owner, president and publisher of *Baseball America*. It had grown and become the premier baseball publication in the country. But it would be difficult to run the newspaper from Canada. It was time to move on. My ownership had taken *BA* as far as possible with limited resources. Now publishing professionals were ready to make the purchase and take the publication to the next level. *Baseball America* had been a major part of my working life. Through the paper I became involved in independent baseball. It had given our organization great visibility in the baseball world. As I had grown up in a newspaper family, it was always a thrill to be part of the publication. The sale was completed in early 2000 at a price of nearly $2 million.

13

Baseball America

One morning in 1981 after stopping by the Durham Bulls' post office box, I found a thin newspaper included in the mail. The name of the publication was the *All-America Baseball News*. The content of the paper was a bit of a mishmash, but it was devoted exclusively to baseball. College baseball news and major league news were emphasized with some minor league information included. Strangely, it was published out of White Rock, British Columbia, not a hotbed of baseball interest. An ad on an interior page for the paper pushed a yearly subscription, and I decided to subscribe. Over the years, other attempts at baseball publications had been tried, but something was unique about this one.

The next few months brought me the biweekly subscription as the newspaper appeared to be finding its footing. But it remained a thin publication with little advertising. It seemed questionable if the paper would make it. I received a call from my baseball maven, Bob Freitas, and during the conversation he began talking about the *All-America Baseball News*. He knew the editor and lamented that the paper might have to go out of business. The editor was a one-man show doing everything from the garage in his home in Canada. Freitas suggested that I should consider buying the newspaper to keep it alive. I was not sure why Freitas was pushing me to buy a newspaper, but his suggestion struck a chord.

For nearly a century, *The Sporting News* had been the publication for all of baseball. Under the Spink family, it was devoted almost entirely to baseball. The family sold the publication in the 1970s and changes were made. It was no longer baseball's special newspaper. But this little paper, the *All-America Baseball News*, had the germ of something special. Could this compete against *The Sporting News*? Was it something even to consider? The idea grew.

The Sporting News

It was on the newsstand at the drugstore in the Summit Shopping Center. For a twelve-year-old obsessed with baseball, it was the equivalent of finding

13. Baseball America

the Dead Sea Scrolls. Was this real? You lifted it gently off the rack. What was inside? You did not know that such a thing existed. It was a tabloid newspaper devoted to nothing but baseball. On the inside were articles on major leaguers and the minor leagues with pages of statistics and box scores. It came out every week, and it was marvelous. It was the Sporting News.

You had to have a copy. You paid your 25 cents and hid it under your shirt. You did not know what your mother would think. The publication was sold on the same row as the girlie magazines, and certainly you couldn't bring one of those home. Was this also taboo? You sneaked it up to your bedroom, closed your door, and let the numbers and standings and every statistic shower over you. Perhaps there were better things in this world, but you could not imagine anything else. When your mother discovered the hidden newsprint, it was not a problem, but how were you to know?

The Sporting News *was known as baseball's bible, and it certainly was your Bible. For the next decade you rushed to the newsstand every week to pick up a copy. Even when you left for college it did not lose its fascination. At a newsstand on Greenmount Avenue in Baltimore, about a mile from the Johns Hopkins campus, you discovered that the weekly edition was delivered at midnight every Saturday. For most college students, Saturday night is a time to drink and party. But for you the highlight was to make the trek to pick up the* Sporting News. *Your roommate thought this strange, but he was an amiable fellow and would make the mile or so walk with you to the newsstand. A truck would arrive punctually at midnight, and a bunch of bound* Sporting News *copies would be thrown off the back bed of the truck. You would rush to the stack and slip out a copy. To appease your roommate, there would be a stop for pancakes at an all-night diner, where you studied the newspaper while he chuckled at his strange roommate.*

Then, as with all things that are perfect, it changed. No longer was it exclusively baseball, and the minor league news and box scores were dropped. You still read it, but not with the regularity that had once been your habit. The joy that had once been present when you opened the pages was gone, but the memories were special.

It was 1981. I had owned the Durham Bulls for one year and that first year was good. My philosophy on making a successful franchise was that it takes at least three years to establish a club in a community. My efforts needed to be directed to the Bulls. And yet, the Freitas call pushed a button. I had loved the *Sporting News*. Baseball needed its own publication. Was this something you really could do? I had no knowledge of the publishing business, and did I even have the time to attempt this? Freitas had given the phone number of the editor. It would not hurt to call and assess the situation.

There's a Bulldozer on Home Plate

The editor's name was Allan Simpson. He was Canadian, originally from Kelowna, British Columbia, but now living in White Rock, B.C. He was married with two children and another on the way. As a kid, he had gotten the baseball bug, and at night, under the covers of his bed, he would try to pick up radio signals of baseball broadcasts that might drift across the border from the U.S. At one point he had worked in baseball, first with the Alaska Goldpanners of the Alaskan Summer Collegiate League and then with the Lethbridge Dodgers of the Pioneer League. But these jobs did not support a family and Allan became an accountant. Every indication was that his accounting career was going well. But at some point in 1980, he decided to start a baseball newspaper. He moved his family to White Rock, close to the U.S. border. With most of his subscription base in the U.S., he needed to mail the publication from a U.S. post office to get reasonable postal rates. Thus, every two weeks he drove across the border to mail issues to his two or three thousand subscribers.

Reaching him on the phone, Allan let me know the situation. He was unable to continue publishing the paper without help and funds. He needed $25,000 to repay his father who had loaned him the money to start, and he needed a U.S. visa. He was willing to move his family to North Carolina if we could work out some financial arrangement and get a visa.

In retrospect, I am not certain what the impulse was to acquire the newspaper. My father had been a newspaperman, a good one, but I had no experience in publications, nor did any of our staff. Allan Simpson was totally dedicated to the paper, but his knowledge of the business end of publishing was limited. Yet, once I had talked with Allan I knew I wanted the paper. It wasn't a business decision. It was a baseball decision. The game needed its own publication, and in those years, my staff and I believed we could do anything that was associated with baseball. Sure, we can publish a baseball newspaper that competes against the Bible of Baseball. Our hubris was growing, matching our enthusiasm. I agreed with Allan on the payment of debts. Now I needed to get a visa to complete the deal. Allan and the newspaper needed to be headquartered in Durham.

My knowledge of immigration was less than my knowledge of publishing, and I called our lawyer, Mr. Mount, to see how to move forward. He knew that the immigration and visa process was not simple, and this was not his specialty. He could direct me to an immigration lawyer, but he suggested that I first go to the U.S. immigration office in Charlotte,

13. Baseball America

North Carolina, to ask for advice on the proper procedures before hiring a lawyer for the formal preparation.

I made the drive to Charlotte. Upon getting to the office, I was given a form to fill out and told to wait. After an hour or so, an immigration official came out and took the form.

I had filled out the information on Allan Simpson and waited to get more details on the visa process. In half an hour, the official returned and handed me a sheet of paper. It was a five-year visa for Simpson. I wanted to question the official how this was possible, obtaining a visa without asking or being asked any questions. I had been told the process was difficult.

However, silence is often the best policy, and I thanked the official and quickly departed. The next day I called Allan to tell him the good news that we had a visa. Our deal was finalized, and he could make the move and come to North Carolina. He was a bit distracted as he informed me that his wife, Jill, was in labor. That day, they had their third child. Apparently, Allan had not kept Jill apprised of all the developments in Durham, and he was hesitant to tell her at this critical time. It was six weeks before he felt comfortable telling her that the family was moving. She did not object.

Within six months Allan was in Durham. The name of the publication was changed to *Baseball America*. Allan settled in the back of the souvenir store and in the early years laid out the paper on nacho boxes. Allan was totally dedicated to the publication and in those first few years worked 80–100 hours a week. Dave Chase took over all business functions, and the Bulls' staff was involved, helping with mailings, circulation, and advertising.

Dave Chase was a recent hire by the Bulls. With the first year's success, we needed more staff, and Dave came up from Anderson, South Carolina, where he had been the GM of the Anderson Braves. I had confidence that someone who could successfully take on the role of a minor league GM could handle any number of jobs. Dave was thrown the *Baseball America* responsibility. Over the years, a dozen different jobs would be thrown at Dave, and he would always rise to the occasion. The old building across the street from the ballpark, our souvenir store and concessions storage space—now named "Ballpark Corner"—became world headquarters for *Baseball America*.

The newspaper grew each year, and circulation, which had been about 3,000 when the paper was purchased, increased to over 40,000 by the end of the 1980s. *Baseball America* looked at itself as the primary

There's a Bulldozer on Home Plate

publisher for almost anything baseball and we soon branched off into other products. The directory for professional baseball since 1911 had been the *Blue Book*, priced in 1981 at over $30 and shipped after the season started. In February 1983, *BA* came out with the *Baseball America Directory* at $3.95 with names, addresses, positions, and schedules for all of major, minor and college baseball. For decades, the *Sporting News* had published the *Baseball Guide*. To counter the *Sporting News*, we came out with the *Baseball America Almanac* which had every statistic for major and minor league baseball in the prior season. Other products such as the *Baseball America Super Register*, the *Encyclopedia of Minor League Baseball*, the *Great Minor League Ballparks Calendar* and a dozen other publications were published by *Baseball America*.

The *Encyclopedia of Minor League Baseball* was a project that I headed. Along with co-editor Lloyd Johnson, one of the nation's great baseball historians, we produced a volume that covered the history of minor league baseball from the 1880s to the present day. It included standings of every minor league that had ever played along with league leaders, attendance figures, and other facts in one volume. *Baseball America* published three of the editions in 1993, 1996, and 2007, as each volume added new information and research. A final edition was published by McFarland in 2023.

As the publication expanded, the staff increased and Allan hired some of the best young baseball writers in the country. There was pride when our writers were hired away by larger publications. *Baseball America* alumni became writers for the *New York Times*, *Sports Illustrated*, ESPN, and other national outlets. Beat writers for major league teams included many writers who had their start in Durham. Some of the best-established baseball writers in the country had columns in the paper. In the early years some of these columnists also wrote for *The Sporting News*. That publication took notice and informed columnists such as Peter Gammons and Terry Pluto that they could not write for both publications. Although *Baseball America* did not have the circulation or pay as well, there was satisfaction when these writers chose *Baseball America* over the *Sporting News*. The good baseball writers desired to write for the pure baseball publication.

Allan Simpson was a perfectionist, and he often found errors in copy or obscure statistics that three proofreaders had missed. Print deadlines were never missed but sometimes the envelope was pushed as Allan made certain everything was perfect. His strength was the baseball draft, the yearly selection of amateur players by major league clubs.

13. **Baseball America**

Scouts of MLB clubs scoured the country looking for top talent. Allan's sources gave him the inside information on this talent and made his list of top prospects in the country a must-read for major league organizations as well as fans. One MLB club, finding the name of a top prospect in *BA* that it thought it had hidden, sent out word to its scouts that if any were discovered talking to *Baseball America*, they would be fired immediately.

Baseball America's growth was steady until the early 1990s. Then, *USA Today*, the national daily newspaper, came out with a new publication, *Baseball Weekly*. Piggybacking on *USA Today*'s reach on the newsstands, *Baseball Weekly* slowed the growth of *BA*. The content of *Baseball Weekly* was almost exclusively major league, and *Baseball America* continued to be the insiders' publication. Then in 1994, Major League Baseball players went out on strike. We were surprised when subscribers called to cancel subscriptions. Fans were mad at baseball and needed to take out their anger on someone. *Baseball America* became the recipient.

When the paper was sold in early 2000, the internet was becoming a factor. In retrospect, it was a fortunate time to get out. Our masthead always read, "Baseball News You Can't Get Anywhere Else." The publication was the only place for minor league stats and standings and other inside information on baseball. As the internet grew and developed, a baseball fan could now find baseball news any time. *Baseball America* had been published every two weeks, and it had to adjust. The paper is now a monthly publication and specializes in prospects and the draft. For the first 19 years, *Baseball America* was built by a dedicated staff in Durham. It was a good run.

14

Quebec

It was another phone call to *Baseball America*. In 1997, a caller inquired about baseball coming to Quebec City. The question was again forwarded to me. This was a similar situation to the calls that had helped start the Northern League four years earlier. But the difference was that, by 1997, several independent leagues were operating in the northeast U.S. that might be a fit for the Canadian city. Always looking for a reason to visit a ballpark, I suggested that a trip might be made to Quebec City to see the stadium, access the potential, and look at alternatives. The caller was positive in his response and arrangements were made for a trip.

While Montréal was the major city in the province of Quebec, Quebec City was the next largest population center and the provincial capital. The city had a good baseball history and for many years had been a member of the Provincial League. In the 1940s, the Provincial League had been an "outlaw" league, hiring players who were banned by the major leagues or signing players under contract to U.S. minor league teams. In 1950, the Provincial League became a member of the National Association and was part of organized baseball. Quebec City became a farm team for the Boston and Milwaukee Braves. After the league folded as a professional league in 1956, it continued as a semi-pro or men's senior league. Then, in 1971, Quebec City came back to organized baseball as a member of the Double-A Eastern League and a farm team of the Montréal Expos. The team drew well in the first few years, but ultimately failed and the franchise folded after the 1977 season.

It was late spring when I made the trip to Quebec and was met at the airport by Jean-François Côté, the individual who had called *Baseball America* a few months earlier. Jeff was involved in all things baseball in the city and was totally enthusiastic. He was very much like the first fans who had called from Northern League cities, and I was hopeful that the situation would be positive in this city. Then I saw the ballpark. Le Stade de Québec had been built in 1939 and the last professional

14. Quebec

game had been played there in 1977. My first impression was that no work had been done on the structure since the last team departed. It was a large concrete building, seating nearly 5,000 fans, but concrete was falling from the front pillars. The ticket booths were in shambles and the interior of the facility was a disaster. A junior team for players ages 16 to 21 still played in the facility, but it was a wonder that the structure had not been condemned. Normally, I could dream when I saw old ballparks. Durham was awful and Duluth was a wreck when I made my first trips to these parks, but I could envision how they might be resurrected. Quebec City (both Quebec and Québec are correct in the bilingual nation) was nowhere close. I toured the ballpark for nearly an hour but found little to recommend. I reluctantly told Jeff the saddest of possible words. It would be impossible for Le Stade to be made suitable for professional baseball.

It was six months later when Jeff Côté called again. He told me that work had started on refurbishing the stadium, and he wondered if I could make another trip to Quebec. I agreed. Upon arrival, I saw that some cleanup of the facility had started, and a fans group had begun painting the seats and the outfield wall. Most importantly, city government, which had ignored the facility for 20 years, saw that the citizens cared about the old park. City officials assured me that money would be available for improvements and repairs if a team was willing to come to the city. The amount of work completed was not impressive, but the spirit in the city was. I began to reconsider.

I could certainly point out negatives for putting a club in the city. First was language. Ninety-five percent of the residents were French-speaking. Would it be possible to run a team in a foreign language? Where would a front-office staff come from? Certainly, I knew of no experienced baseball front-office folks who spoke French. The team would be in a foreign country. How difficult would it be to get visas? The city had just lost an NHL team, the Québec Nordiques, one of the most beloved teams in all of hockey. A minor-league International Hockey League team moved to Quebec following the Nordiques and failed miserably. I met with the American owners of that team, the Quebec Rafales, and they warned me to stay away from Quebec, saying it was folly for an American to operate in the francophone community. Would the sports media welcome an independent minor-league baseball team? Would there be local ownership available? And what was the city's real commitment to Le Stade?

With all the negatives, I pushed forward. There was something

There's a Bulldozer on Home Plate

special about Quebec. The team needed a league, and the Northeast League was available. League directors had contacted me about taking over as commissioner, and with Dan Moushon, the league president, overseeing the day-to-day operations, the league would be stabilized. I was aware that ownership would be difficult to find, but I was prepared to be on-site and running the club until a local owner was found. It had been nearly ten years since I had operated a team myself, and it might be good to try it one more time. In regard to the language, I had an ace in my back pocket. Michelle's first language was French.

Michelle grew up in northern Maine with seven brothers and two sisters in a village named Frenchville. She spoke only French until she attended a school where nuns would punish those who did not speak English. During one of my early trips to Quebec City to determine if baseball could work, Michelle accompanied me and fell in love with the city. With all the French around, it was as if she had come home. She was worried that her Frenchville *patois* would not be accepted, but no one noticed. The Québécois loved Americans who tried to speak French, and hers was excellent. Mine was nonexistent.

My plans were not to have Michelle work at the ballpark. If we were to move with the kids to the city, someone would need to handle the day-to-day operations of keeping a household going. That would be her role. But how was I going to run a ballclub in French? Jeff Côté, who had first called, was ready to come on board with the new team, and his English was excellent. He could translate for me. But a club would need more employees than Jeff. The need was for French speakers who understood baseball.

In the summer of 1998 with the probability of putting a team in Quebec getting closer, I was making the rounds of the Northern League when I stopped in Madison and visited with "Dirty Al" who was managing the Black Wolf. He had heard of the project in Quebec.

"Miles, I got just the person for you for that team in Canada."

"Who's that, Al?"

"My best pitcher, Michel Laplante. He could work in your front office and pitch for you."

"Al, I'm not big on players in the front office. They don't really understand the work involved."

"Don't worry, Miles. This is a quality guy and you'll like him. Just talk to him."

I talked with Michel Laplante, and Al was correct. He was a quality individual. For part of the game, I sat with his wife, Francine, who was seven months pregnant. She also made a positive impression. They were high school sweethearts who had married young, and she had been with Michel on his minor league journey. He had pitched professionally for seven seasons, including one year in Taiwan, but now with a baby on the way, it was time to settle down. They had both learned English in the crucible of minor-league baseball travel, and their dream was to be able to work in the U.S. But Michel's ballplaying visa did not work for other jobs, and it appeared that the two would return to Val-d'Or, Quebec, where the only jobs were in the mines. They both appeared excited about a venture in Quebec City.

One other francophone ballplayer was in the Northern League that season, and he also played for Madison. His name was Stéphane Dionne. He was a backup catcher with marginal ability but had managed to stick in independent baseball for a couple of seasons because of his outgoing personality. Stéphane had shown up at one of the first Northern League tryout camps in 1993. The camp was in Florida and he was sleeping in the back of his VW Beetle. His English was limited and he was not going to make a club, but Marv Goldklang was so impressed with the eagerness of Stéphane that he suggested that the young catcher

Michel Laplante, the first player signed to a 1999 Québec Capitales contract. He would be sold to the Montréal Expos and later would return to Les Capitales as a player, coach, manager and ultimately president of the franchise.

There's a Bulldozer on Home Plate

come to St. Paul to be the bullpen catcher. He was part of the magical first year with the Saints. At the end of the seasons, one of the coaches with the Duluth team, who was also head baseball coach at Oklahoma City University, offered him a scholarship to play baseball at OCU. Stéphane was the first in his family to attend college and he worked hard. The Oklahoma City bombing took place while he was in school, and he became the correspondent for French-language Canadian media during the tragic episode.

Four years later, upon graduation, Stéphane headed back to St. Paul in the role of backup catcher. Unfortunately, he was in the U.S. on a student visa, and returning with the team from a series in Winnipeg, he was taken off the bus at the border by U.S. immigration. His career with the Saints was over. For the following season, he was issued a valid visa to play in Madison. He worked in the Madison front office in the winter and set up a successful reading program for elementary school students. Each child who read ten books during the school year would be given tickets to Black Wolf games. The promotion worked well. But by mid-season, with Stéphane's average hovering around .150, it was clear that his career would not be long and that meant returning home to Rimouski. A job in Quebec City was more appealing.

It was a no-brainer to hire both players. I needed French speakers who understood independent baseball. Both qualified and if they didn't work out in the front office, we still had two spots filled on the roster. When the Madison season was over, they both were on their way to Quebec.

The final decision on Quebec was made that summer. I had an option on a team that had been in Bangor, Maine, and had failed the year before. The price was $190,000. The Northeast League was eager to have Quebec, and I would be commissioner. No buyer was willing to take a chance on a Quebec team, and I would need to be the sole owner. Bulls' stockholders were not eager to come along on this venture. Michelle had found a house to rent near the Plains of Abraham. The kids were 14 and 12, tough years to take them out of a school they had attended since the first grade. Both reluctantly gave an OK. Michelle and I hoped that it would be a good experience for them. With few English-language schools in the city, it would have been a tough transition to put them in a situation with no English. Luckily there was an English-language school near the rental house. The family moved up to Quebec in late August.

It was the start of a love affair with the city. For the next twenty

14. Quebec

years, this would be our second home. Quebec City was such a beautiful city with history on every street. With the home near the Plains of Abraham, I could walk almost anywhere, and it was a city made for walking. The city celebrated every season of the year. Christmas decorations were kept up for months, and the winter carnival was a special time with ice sculpting, ice castles, dog sledding and more. Coming to the city, I was worried about snow and driving. In North Carolina with two inches of snow, every school was closed for a week and the cities shut down. In Quebec City it seemed to snow most every night, but by the morning, the streets were clean, and driving was never a problem. The kids walked to school, and only once was school closed for a half day because of a particularly heavy blizzard. Spring was late, but the city blossomed with tulips and daffodils. The summer music festivals were almost weekly and the temperature in the summer was always comfortable. In the fall, the cruise ships stopped for the fall foliage, and thousands of tourists came ashore to view the leaves and visit the little shops that surround the port. There was so much to love about Quebec.

The city had reawakened to baseball, and the first year with the Québec Capitales was exceptional. On the field the club finished second in the division with a 43–43 record. The best player was Michel Laplante, who compiled an 11–2 record and was sold to the Montréal Expos at the end of the season. Six Québécois players were signed by Les Capitales and all contributed on the field. I always believed that it was important to have players that the fans could identify with, and the fans responded well to the French-speaking players. It also helped with the two daily French-language newspapers, and the coverage given to the team was excellent.

After the first season, we bought the home we were renting and seriously considering making it our full-time residence. Our son Hoffman adjusted well and he loved the freedom of the city. It was a safe city, and he could take the bus at night to hockey games and other events by himself. We did not worry. He played sports at school, became proficient in French, and was eager to enroll in a French-language school in his second year. For our daughter, Claire, it was a different story. Seventh-grade girls are a cliquish group which made things difficult. Academically she was a top student, but the school was not her favorite. When we started talking about staying permanently in Quebec, Claire announced that we could stay, but she was going back to Durham whether we came with her or not. Her arguments won out.

The team manager the first year was Jay Ward. Jay was the perfect choice for Quebec. He played fifteen seasons in the minors with a couple of cups of coffee in the big leagues. He had managed for ten seasons and had been the major-league hitting coach for the Montréal Expos for several seasons. He was hard-nosed, operated by-the-book and had the players act professionally. With an independent team, laxness could be a problem, but Jay would not allow this and the fans appreciated his intensity. It is not a usual requirement in professional clubhouses, but he demanded that a player's locker be neat at all times. Included in that directive was the stipulation that coat hangers be all turned in the same direction. My first reaction was that the direction of coat hangers was not something that I had ever heard of as a priority in baseball. I asked Jay about this politely (to repeat, Jay was hard-nosed), but he was glad to answer. He agreed that coat hangers were a little thing, but he wanted his players to be conscious of the little things. Hitting the cut-off man on throws from the outfield was a little thing, but he wanted his players to perform correctly on every play. He felt the tone was set in the clubhouse and carried over to the playing field.

In one particular game, the opposing pitcher threw and intentionally hit one of the Quebec batters. Jay then instructed his pitcher to throw at one of the opposing batters. The Quebec pitcher refused. He explained that once he had hurt someone in a fight and never wanted to injure anyone again. Apparently, this did not sit well with Jay. Jay believed that you protect your teammates. He immediately took the pitcher out of the game. After the game, he called the pitcher into his office and released him. Words ensued and a fight broke out between the 62-year-old manager and the 23-year-old pitcher. When it was over, an ambulance was called and the pitcher was taken to the hospital. Details were vague, but the pitcher was having trouble breathing and those who broke up the fight intimated that the manager's hands near the pitcher's throat might have caused the breathing problem. The pitcher was released from the hospital the next day and was quickly signed by another team in the league.

Jay had three good years in Quebec, but in the end he decided not to return when the fans turned on him. He had released a popular Québécois catcher who was doing well. The player and Jay did not see eye-to-eye, and when he was released, the fan base and media took exception. His time was over with the Capitales, but I was glad Jay was the first manager. He set the tone for Les Capitales, and his professionalism and intensity remained part of the team culture (except for the coat hangers) for the next two decades.

14. Quebec

Le Stade, Quebec City, Quebec. Built in 1939, the stadium has been home to Les Capitales de Québec since 1999. It is the exact same design as the stadium in Trois-Rivières with both facilities being funded by the provincial government. The grandstand seats approximately 4,500. It is set in Parc Victoria, about a mile from the historic city center.

The fans in Quebec were special and the most enthusiastic I had ever dealt with at the minor league level. A dance contest between innings encouraged fans in different sections of the ballpark to dance to lively music. Everyone danced and it was great fun. The fans sang along to French songs played between innings, and our picnic area became a lively pregame social hour. The phrase "joie de vivre" fit. I wondered if this was a Canadian thing, but that was not the case. Winnipeg opened a new, beautiful stadium the same year with record crowds of over 6,000 a game. The ballpark was the place to be in Winnipeg. But the noise level in Quebec was twice as high with half the crowd. The English-speaking Winnipeggers stayed in their seats, cheering and clapping politely after good plays. The contrast with Quebec fans was striking.

When the Montréal Expos came into existence in 1969, baseball interest in the province and in all of Canada grew tremendously. More kids started playing baseball at the youth level, and quality players were developed and signed by major league organizations. Several of those players made the big leagues, including Éric Gagné, who won the National League's Cy Young award in 2003 as the best pitcher in the league. With the interest in the Capitales high, drafted affiliated players from the province came to play in Quebec after they were released. It became important to end a playing career in Quebec. Even Éric Gagné pitched for Quebec after his outstanding career with the Los Angeles Dodgers. Each season, at least four or five French-speaking players were on the roster and in some years, as many as nine or ten. With these quality players on the team, at one point Les Capitales won five straight pennants.

Players loved playing in Quebec. The crowds were large and the living accommodation special. Downtown Quebec City was expensive and most years the team made arrangements for accommodations at Stoneham, a ski resort about ten miles outside of the city. The ski season was over, and the condos were generally open. Some years during spring training in mid–May, workouts would be finished by noon, and with snow remaining on the ski slopes, players skied in the afternoon. The women of Quebec were also an attraction, and each year players fell in love and tried to stay year-round. But visas expired at the end of the season, and players reluctantly had to leave. A few were able to stay, marrying local girls and becoming Canadian citizens.

One who stayed, married and became a proud Canadian was Eddie Lantigua, a third baseman. Eddie originally signed with the Dodgers and reached as high as Double-A before he was released. He bounced around independent baseball for a few years, but when he came to Quebec, he found his home. Eddie was originally from the Dominican Republic, but prospects for a successful future in that country were limited. For nine seasons, he played for the Capitales and set records for home runs and RBIs. He married a Quebec girl and raised a family,

14. Quebec

becoming a local hero. Eddie would tell other players, "This is my big leagues and I am going to make the most of it." For 16 seasons, he played independent baseball, but he always came back to Quebec.

I spent 11 years as owner of Les Capitales de Québec. Every year I hoped to find a buyer. A few tire-kickers emerged, but nothing developed. The business did not start making money until the year Éric Gagné came to pitch, but the losses, while manageable, built up over the first eight seasons. Finally in 2011, I was able to complete a sale. The sale price was $950,000, which made up for the losses with a little left over for profit. In the years that I was owner, I never took a salary, but it didn't matter. The Quebec run was a good one.

The new owner, Jean Tremblay, was not a baseball fan, but he believed the team was good for the city. He was the owner of a lawn care company with nearly 50 franchises around the province. Jean owned several other businesses, including some in Florida. Although very successful, he was not well-known. The ballclub changed that. When the premier of the province or the mayor came to a game, they would sit with Jean. Charity golf tournaments wanted him to play in their events. While the ballclub was not a big profit center for him, his ownership drove many to sign up for his grass maintenance plan. He was the perfect local owner. He named Michel Laplante as president of the team, and under Michel's direction, the team thrived.

15

What's a Road Team?

While Quebec was occupying much of my time, I remained commissioner of the two leagues. The winter months were spent in Durham, a time when the league office sets regulations and policies for the coming season. League meetings were held in the fall when important league decisions were made. With my involvement in the Northeast League, the Northern League had given the Northeast League permission to use the name "Northern League East" for a four-year trial period. The Northeast League did not have the strong cities and good facilities that now were the signature of the Northern League, but we hoped that the association would help strengthen the cities and facilities in the east. While there was growth in the east, by the end of the 2002 season, the Northern League voted not to continue with the Northeast League.

With my involvement in the Northeast and Quebec, it was time to leave. I submitted my resignation to the Northern League. The Northern League was strong with ten cities, and the original owners other than the St. Paul group were gone. At the final league meeting of the Northern League that I chaired, nine lawyers were present. The league had no major problems, but the success and value of the franchises convinced some members of the need for legal representation. Several of the new ownership groups were headed by lawyers. My view of the legal profession remained mixed, and the legal presence at the meeting helped make my decision easier. I could help the Northeast League. The Northern League was solid and could go its own way.

In the nine years of my commissionership, the growth of the Northern League had been impressive. The league's schedule had expanded from 72 to 100 games. Multi-million-dollar stadiums were being built by cities across the Midwest to gain entry into the league. Of the original six, St. Paul, Sioux City and Sioux Falls remained. Fargo-Moorhead's entry into the league in 1996 with a new facility kicked off a stadium building boom for the league. While Duluth operated in 2002, the franchise had committed to move into a new facility in Kansas City, Kansas,

15. What's a Road Team?

the following season. In 1999, Winnipeg moved from the old football stadium to a new downtown park seating nearly 7,000, cementing the Goldeyes as one of the league's attendance leaders. Lincoln's entry into the league in 2001 in a stadium shared with the University of Nebraska was a huge success. The move of the Thunder Bay team to Schaumburg, Illinois, in 1998 opened the Chicago market for the league, leading to new franchises in Gary, Indiana, and Joliet, Illinois. These cities brought the league's membership to ten for the 2002 season.

The Northeast League showed some growth starting in 2002. The addition of Brockton, Massachusetts, that year in a new stadium was a bright spot. The Quebec team and the New Jersey Jackals, the latter playing out of Montclair, New Jersey, were both solid franchises, but the league had gone to many former Eastern League and Atlantic League cities, and these teams struggled. The facilities were old, and replacing a failed team was never a great way to start. The cities in many cases were old Rust Belt towns with a fraying sense of community. The league survived, but movement of franchises was frequent and the ability to get quality ownership lagged.

Allentown, Pennsylvania, was one of the cities that failed. The owner had placed the team in an old softball facility, barely adequate for any sort of team. He kept the team alive for seven seasons in hopes that a new facility might be approved by city leaders. In May 2004 with about two weeks to go before the start of the season, he called the league office to inform us that he would not operate unless the league provided significant funds to help him through the season. It should be mentioned that the owner was a personal injury attorney. He believed that a new stadium was close to a reality in Allentown, and he demanded the league subsidize his operation until a facility was constructed. With the season so close to starting, he knew the league had no time to find a new city to replace Allentown. He also knew league members would lose a significant number of home dates that would be costly if Allentown did not play. The word "extortion" came to mind. Dan Moushon and I quickly went to work, and within three days a road team, the Aces, was ready to go.

At that time, road teams were almost never seen in baseball, and over decades of minor league baseball there had been few. Simply put, road teams played all their games on the road. There was no home base, and the Aces took over the Ambassadors' dates on the schedule, simply moving the games originally scheduled for Allentown to the visiting team's park. Having to pay for 100 days of hotels, buses, meals and salaries was expensive, but the costs were split among the seven other teams. In this case, it protected the league cities for their scheduled home dates plus gave each city six or seven additional home dates. For cities that drew well, it could be a small profit center. The worry was finding players, but enough players with experience wanted to play, no matter what the circumstance, and the team roster was quickly filled. Some players actually liked the situation of a good hotel to stay in every night and meal money for all games. Invariably, road teams had losing records, but the team was reasonably competitive, as the Aces finished with a record of 28–64.

The Allentown owner was enraged and, as lawyers are wont to do, he sued. He argued that we illegally took his franchise. Legal costs were high and went on for years, but before the suit reached trial, the lawyer and his wife were killed in a small airplane crash. They left no heirs. Even with that, his lawyer continued the lawsuit until the league settled and paid his firm enough to go away.

In the aftermath of the Allentown debacle and lawsuit and on the advice of our lawyers, the Northeast League dissolved and the remaining members formed a new league for the 2005 season: the Canadian-American Association, or Can-Am League for short. The Can-Am League had been a professional league that operated from 1938 to 1955 with some of the same cities. The new league would have ties to a part of that baseball history.

A former Can-Am city, Ottawa, Ontario, entered the league in 2008. Ottawa had been a member of the Triple-A International League from 1993 through 2007. The franchise was very successful in the early years, playing in a new 10,000-seat faculty. In the first season, the Ottawa Lynx led all minor league teams in attendance with over 600,000 spectators. But attendance started falling, and by 2007, the total was less than 2,000 a game. In 2008, the team moved to the new ballpark in Allentown and enjoyed spectacular success. Part of the reason for the failure of the Triple-A club in Ottawa was due to the league schedule that opened in early April. Ottawa does not begin warming until late May, and playing baseball in frigid temperatures makes the spectator experience a bit testy. Many games were postponed due to snow, and on one occasion, a rain shower caused a four-game delay. The field was covered with a tarp to protect against the rain. When the rain stopped, the temperature dropped, and before the tarp could be rolled back up, the rain froze on the tarp. It was four days later when the sheet of ice melted and the tarp became flexible enough to roll. With the

15. What's a Road Team?

Can-Am starting in late May, the belief was that a franchise had a good chance for success.

A local owner was found in Ottawa, a successful high-tech businessman, and it appeared that Ottawa would be a strong addition to the league. Unfortunately, the owner ignored advice and began spending money on projects that would best have been delayed. At the end of the season, he announced he had lost over a million dollars and would not operate in 2009 unless the city and the league met some unrealistic demands. At the annual league meeting that fall, the league took his franchise, and he sued. The suit, which centered around laws on international arbitration, ultimately went to the Supreme Court of Canada where the league won a unanimous decision. But a potential good city, Ottawa, was lost.

The first decade of the 21st century was a fluid time in independent baseball as leagues were changing. Start-up leagues became less frequent, and existing leagues were solidifying. The Durham office became headquarters for several additional teams and leagues. In 2001, talks were started to take over management of the Central League, formerly the Texas-Louisiana League. That league was now owned by Horn Chen, a Chicago businessman and minor league hockey owner. I knew Horn from the East Coast Hockey League. He renamed the league the Central League to match his hockey league of the same name. He was looking for new leadership, and I became commissioner in 2002. The Central League was an eight-team league with some good markets, principally Ft. Worth and Amarillo. Several new ballparks had been built for clubs. It had potential.

By 2005, the office in Durham was running two leagues, the Can-Am and Central, with a total of 16 teams; an Appalachian League team in Burlington; a concession company, Baseball Concessions, Inc.; and the club in Quebec which I was running on-site. It all worked because Dan Moushon in the Durham office was efficient, organized, and simply good. The only other person in the office was a part-timer who handled the media, night-time distribution of scores and wrap-ups, and assorted clerical tasks dealing with player contracts. Off-site, the umpire-in-chief, Kevin Winn, supervised umpires and handled on-field problems. I dealt with ownership and Dan handled the GMs.

During that period, summer college baseball became part of our operations. College baseball's regular season ended in mid–May. Championship tournaments extended the season for a few teams into June, but the bulk of players were idle and looking for a place to play.

There's a Bulldozer on Home Plate

Summer college baseball had shown an amazing level of growth as players were eager to continue their development over the summer. Most summer college leagues were wood-bat leagues. During the regular college seasons, these players used aluminum bats, but if they hoped to play professionally, they needed to become accustomed to wood bats. These summer leagues provided that experience. The players were not paid, and some leagues actually charged the players for participation. If a team could draw 400–500 fans a night, breaking even was possible.

Our office received a call from a league that needed ownership for a team in Little Falls, New York. The population of the city was only around 5,000, but it had at one time in the 1980s been a farm club of the Mets. The ballpark was small but neat and clean. There would be no charge for the franchise. The league needed the market to fill out its schedule. The key to success is having a quality front office, and we had no one available to go to Little Falls. As we discussed the possibility, Dan brought up Hoffman, my son, as a potential GM. Hoffman had graduated from college and was working in the sports information department of the University at Albany. He had obviously grown up knowing the minors but never worked in the business. Dan thought he could do it, and when I asked Hoffman if he was interested, he replied in the affirmative.

Hoffman did a good job in Little Falls, and that fall we sold it to local interests for a small profit. The next year Hoffman went to Atlantic City in the Can-Am League as an assistant, and the following year went to Elmira, New York, to be GM of another college team we had purchased. Hoffman set up a good operation in Elmira, and at the end of the season, having proven it was a viable college market, we sold it for another small profit. That was the last year for our organization in summer college baseball. We needed to concentrate on the independent teams.

Hoffman followed up with a year in Brockton. Brockton had been one of the bright lights of the Northeast League when the new ballpark opened but had fallen off tremendously. For Hoffman, Brockton was his last stop in baseball. I had sent him to clubs that struggled in less-than-ideal markets. He always did a good job, but he was burnt out. Ultimately, he went back to one of his favorite cities, Quebec City; married a Canadian girl; and is doing well outside of baseball.

In 2005, several owners in the Northern League approached me about their unhappiness with the direction of that league. The league had been through several commissioners, and inexperienced ownership

15. What's a Road Team?

made it a difficult league to run. Could I do anything? The three original franchises of the Northern League, St. Paul, Sioux Falls, and Sioux City, all wanted out, along with the Lincoln club, which had top-flight ownership. I liked these folks and wanted to help, but four clubs were not enough for a league. At the same time, I was experiencing problems in the Central League. The original owners of the Texas-Louisiana League formed a new league, the United League, and had been encouraging the defection of Central League teams. This was creating a difficult situation.

The solution was to form a new league combining the four Northern League cities with five of the Central League teams, letting the others defect to the United. With the addition of a new team in St. Joseph, Missouri, we now had a ten-team league with two divisions. The geography was stretched, but with the two divisions rarely meeting, a workable schedule was possible. The new league took the name of the American Association. The American Association had historically been one of the best Triple-A leagues in minor league baseball. Its history dated back to 1901 and lasted until 1997 when the Triple-A leagues reorganized. St. Paul was a charter member, and at one point Ft. Worth was in the league. The name was a natural, and it had not been protected by Minor League Baseball. It worked.

Ultimately, the Northern League dissolved, and in 2011 Winnipeg, Fargo-Moorhead, Gary, and Kansas City joined the American Association, making that league even stronger. The league at one point stretched from Winnipeg, Manitoba, to Laredo, Texas. Almost every city had built a new ballpark for its franchise. For the next decade, it was arguably the top league in independent baseball and the St. Paul franchise was always ranked near the top of all minor league clubs.

I would often laughingly say that the only good thing about being a commissioner of a baseball league was that the commissioner's signature was on the baseball. My job was to hold the league together, to enforce the rules, to solve the problems of eight or ten teams whose owners were successful businessmen and were not used to having someone tell them what to do. A league had a set of written rules that needed to be enforced. Just as on the field where the game was governed by the official rule book, the league constitution and by-laws set forth rules that owners must follow. Generally, this worked. As commissioner, it was never good to deviate from the league regulations.

Van Schley had been one of my close baseball contacts and friends. He was part of all of the baseball ventures from the Durham Bulls to

There's a Bulldozer on Home Plate

independent baseball. To help the league, he invested in a Northeast League team called the Catskill Cougars. The ballpark was located in the wilderness near Monticello, N.Y., in a market that was not big enough to support a team. He was aware of the limitations but knew a new market might be available in the next few years. Ultimately, the team was able to move to a new facility in Brockton, Massachusetts. The franchise became an immediate success and Van brought several significant investors with him. For the next four years, it was the most successful franchise in the league and with Ed Nottle as manager, it was a special success story in a New England industrial city that had fallen on hard times. But Brockton was not a glamor city, and the front-office staff changed every year or so. The continuity that was needed for a good minor-league operation was not there. The attendance started to decline, and what was once a gem of the independent leagues became a question mark.

Van was a 25 percent owner in the team, and as the losses started to mount, cash calls were issued to stockholders. Van was one of the few who responded. His financial advisor told him he should exit this investment. At the end of the 2011 season, he asked for a little time to try to sell the team. League rules stipulated that a team must give a definite answer by early October if it was going to operate the following season. Van was not prepared to make this commitment. He asked for more time to try to solve Brockton's troubles. He felt that his request was not out of line and that, as one of the founders of the independent movement, he should be given some consideration.

It was my job as commissioner to enforce the rules. The bylaws stated that if a team was not prepared to operate, the franchise and Van's $200,000 letter of credit must be taken. It was clear what I should do, but Van was not an ordinary owner. He had been in independent baseball for 30 years and helped pave the way for its success. Perhaps I could have pushed the directors to waive the bylaws and work with Van on a solution, but I did not. The rules were clear. I took his franchise and the letter of credit. I upheld the rules and lost a friend. My name on a baseball was little consolation.

16

Ottawa

When the remaining clubs from the Northern League came over in 2011 to join the American Association, it solidified and stabilized the league. Nine franchises from the 2012 season still remained through the 2019 season. The Texas clubs saw considerable movement, but the Northern clubs were stable with the league operating as a 12-team league during most of those years. The situation in the Can-Am League was much different, and the league fought to stay alive. Rockland County, New York, entered with a new ballpark in 2011 and the league operated with seven teams and a road team that season. But two clubs failed at the conclusion of the season, and for the next three years, the Can-Am operated as a five- or four-team league. The only salvation for these teams was the American Association. The two leagues agreed to play an interlocking schedule in those years. As commissioner, I encouraged this schedule—probably pushed it more than was wise—even though it entailed airplane travel between the leagues. The cost of air travel for minor league teams was usually prohibitive, but it kept the Can-Am alive. Having just sold the Quebec club in 2011, I could not let that league die with a new owner in Quebec just getting his feet wet. The American Association saved the Can-Am.

It was important for the Can-Am to find new cities, but few were available. The league had lost 11 cities since its formation in 2005 and few of these cities sought to return. Weak ownership had saddled cities with debts, and clubs in two cities, Worcester and Nashua, failed before the season's end. Nashua had problems with a bulldozer and Worcester was bedeviled by a constable. It was never easy for the Durham office.

conversation between league president and commissioner

"We've got a problem in Worcester. The team doesn't have any uniforms."

"Of course they have uniforms. They played in them last night."

There's a Bulldozer on Home Plate

"They don't have them today. A constable came to the ballpark and confiscated them for non-payment of debts in town."

"The owner's broke, but why did the law have to confiscate uniforms? If they can't play games, they can't draw fans and sell tickets, and then they won't have any money to pay off the debts."

"Some lawyer is trying to grandstand. She pressed charges today."

"Ok, do we have any solutions? They certainly can't afford to buy new uniforms."

"We have some of the road team uniforms that we aren't using this year. They're stored in Brockton. I think we can get someone from the Brockton front office to drive them over in time for tonight's game."

"The uniforms say 'Grays' on them. Will that work?"

"It'll have to. We'll just change the name of the team for the rest of the season. It's not pretty, but the situation in Worcester isn't pretty."

"OK. I'll drive down tomorrow and try to work things out."

It was my task to find new markets. I spent considerable time working on Montréal. The city lost the Expos in 2004, and it was a major market with a good core of fans. The problem was always that there was no suitable ballpark, not even a good recreation facility. At least three major suburbs of Montréal had serious interest in building a facility, but none of these potential sites ever materialized. The league added Trois-Rivières, Québec, in 2013. The population base was lower than I might have wanted, but city leaders desired to compete with Quebec City 75 miles away. Enthusiasm was strong in the city, and the league needed members.

In 2013, I began receiving calls from Ottawa. The city had operated in the league in 2008 and failed with poor ownership. The market and ballpark were still excellent, but I doubted the ability to bring the city to the Can-Am. A Double-A Eastern League team was interested in moving to the city and it appeared the Toronto Blue Jays would be the major league affiliate. The Blue Jays, the only MLB club in Canada, had a huge following and would have great appeal in Ottawa. Community interest was high, and it was unlikely the Can-Am League would be able to compete against the Eastern League's proposal. City officials were seriously considering the Eastern League and were estimating the costs of bringing the Double-A team to Ottawa. The city issued an RFQ (Request for

16. Ottawa

Trois-Rivières, Quebec City. Le Stade Fernand-Bernard was built in 1939 with the same design and architecture of Le Stade in Quebec City. The two facilities are virtually identical. The ballpark was built for the team to play in the Provincial League, and the city has hosted teams in that league, the Can-Am League, the Eastern League, and now the Frontier League.

Qualifications) to solicit proposals for a lease on the stadium. RFQs (or RFPs, Requests for Proposals) are procedures that cities are required to follow to show that bidding on a project is a fair and open process, even when city fathers privately know who is going to be selected.

The Can-Am League was sent an RFQ by the city as a potential applicant. It was a detailed document that I believed would be a waste of time to fill out. News reports from Ottawa kept indicating that the Eastern League was a lock with ownership headed by Nolan Ryan, the Hall of Fame pitcher. Ryan was involved in other minor league franchises, and he had the clout and money to submit a winning bid. The deadline for submission was early August. The RFQ remained sitting on my desk.

In mid–July, I received a phone call from a friend in Ottawa whom I had met when the league placed a team in the city five years earlier. He worked for the federal government but knew the politics of the city. He asked if I had received the RFQ and what I was going to do. I let him know that I thought it was pointless to go through the charade of filling it out. I believed the deal was done. We chatted and he began pushing me to submit the document. "You never know what will happen, Miles. You've got nothing to lose by sending it in." Did he know something I didn't know? I filled out the document and sent it in. My submission was mediocre at best, but I could tell league directors that the effort had been made.

It was surprising when a few weeks after the deadline I received phone calls from staff in Ottawa city government asking for more details on the submission. It was not clear why they were asking, but I followed through on the requests. The phone calls kept coming with more questions, and it now was becoming evident that the Can-Am League was in the running for the lease. Officials asked that I come to Ottawa to tour the stadium and give them an idea on specific improvements the league would need. I knew the stadium from our operation in 2008, but I made the trip to Ottawa. After a tour of the facility, I was impressed that the ballpark remained in good shape. I did not ask for major improvements but did request maintenance on areas of the ballpark that had deteriorated.

I was shocked in early October when it was announced that the Can-Am League had been chosen by the city of Ottawa to be the group to negotiate a new lease. Later I found out that the Eastern League group had requested nearly $40 million in improvements. It was greedy, and when the news came that it had lost the bid, it returned and greatly lowered its requests for improvements. It was too late. Over the next few months negotiations were started on a lease with play scheduled to start in the 2015 season.

This was all good news for the Can-Am League. The league had only four teams for 2014, and it gave hope for survival. The overriding problem was that without ownership for the franchise, the lease needed to be completed. I would be the one to negotiate a lease. It was always best if an owner could make specific needs known. However, the league had 18 months to find an owner, and we certainly could work out a lease that might be transferred. Finding owners for Canadian clubs had proven difficult in the past, but this was too good a market for a potential owner to ignore. I was wrong.

As the months went by, it was clear that the league would not find local or outside ownership. The citizens of Ottawa remembered the failure of the Triple-A club and the Can-Am in the market. Even a semi-pro club in the Intercounty League had failed. To be successful, the Can-Am League needed to get the operation off the ground and running. By early

16. Ottawa

2014 with no ownership on the horizon, I began putting my own funds into the club, hiring staff and making arrangements to begin operations, thinking that I should be able to get my money back from the franchise fee when the club was sold.

Running a club was seductive and exciting as I made plans that led to Opening Day. As I worked the operation, the idea started growing. Could I own and operate this team? Ideally, we would find good ownership, but the prospect was dim. The league really needed Ottawa, and I had funded clubs before for the league in Rochester, Madison, Duluth and Quebec. My loans and investments had been repaid. However, at age 70 I was past the time when anyone should be spending 14-hour days running around a ballpark. But I looked at the Ottawa market and saw more potential than I had seen in any of my previous teams. The market had over 1,200,000 in population. I had never operated in a city that large. The ballpark was beautiful, built in 1993, with a great location right off the major highway in the city. The capacity was over 10,000, too much for a minor league stadium, but I certainly could manage that disadvantage. The stadium had revenue streams that were not part of any of my previous operations. There were 32 skyboxes that could be sold at $10,000 a box. The city was giving the team naming rights which could run well over $100,000 a year. There were 800 paid parking spaces. The hockey club was charging $11 for parking. I would charge $5 which would mean an extra $4,000 a night in revenue. The elements were right.

Of the teams that I had owned, three clicked. My other operations were successful, but the three that clicked boomed with attendance and interest far higher than expected. A good operator will have this happen maybe once in a career, but with the Québec Capitales, the Raleigh Ice-Caps, and the Durham Bulls, everything fell perfectly into place. They clicked. Could I make it happen one more time? The Triple-A club in the final years had an excellent GM and good ownership but failed. Was I better? Was ego getting in the way? Was this a dream I needed to take a pass on?

On the other hand, did I have a choice? My name was on the lease, and the other owners in the league weren't going to subsidize this team. I could walk away, but that wasn't really an option. I had a good reputation in baseball. I had gone to the Durham Bulls' stockholders to see if they would take another chance, but it was past the time where they would take a flier on another ball club. This would have to be mine alone.

There's a Bulldozer on Home Plate

The lease negotiations were not easy and I signed a document that was more expensive than any previous lease I had ever signed. The amount was over $400,000 a year. My Quebec lease was less than $50,000. But I tried to justify the Ottawa lease. The city was taking care of everything: all electricity (colloquially referred to as "hydro" in Ontario) and water costs. The annual hydro bill for the Triple-A club was over $200,000 a year. The groundskeeping expense, which included a full-time crew of four, was the responsibility of the city. That cost would have been at least another $150,000. And the city was doing most of the cleanup and all of the maintenance. To top it off, it was spending over $1 million to get the ballpark in shape for the opening season. And the club had all concessions, naming rights, parking and suites. It could work if the team drew enough people. The goal was 2,500 fans a night, not impossible.

With a year to go until the opener, I was spending almost all of my time in Ottawa. Things were falling in place. I did not yet have a GM but had hired several good local folks to start operations. There were some negatives, but I had figured that surely these could be overcome. Media coverage was one worry. The Ottawa Senators were the city's NHL team, and understandably, most of the coverage would go to its one major league team. But this was a winter sport and baseball could be the summertime option. More worrisome was the opening of a new CFL team, the Ottawa Redblacks. The city had been without professional football for over a decade, and $400 million was being spent to upgrade Lansdowne Park, the longtime football facility. The football ownership was also fielding a professional soccer team in its stadium. But this competition should not have been too much of an obstacle. The football team played at home only once every two weeks, and the soccer crowd was very different from a baseball crowd.

By the fall, operations were in full swing. I hired a Canadian to be GM. He had been working for a university athletic department in Vancouver. He had no experience in baseball, but he had the passion and came highly recommended. I named a local political operative as president. It was not a paid position, and he still kept his regular job. He would give us a face in the community with great contacts. He had been the leader to bring the Eastern League to the city, taking pledges for a reported 3,000 season tickets for that team, and if he could do anywhere close to that amount for us, it would be a huge plus. We named the team the Ottawa Champions. In a market that was one-third French-speaking, it was important that our name worked in both

16. Ottawa

languages, and "Champions" had the same meaning in both English and French.

In the plans for the operation of the franchise, I wanted to make certain the Quebec community was included. The city of Gatineau, Quebec, with a population of over 300,000, was just across the river from Ottawa, less than three miles from the ballpark. We needed to be bilingual and make the francophone community feel welcome. Prior operations might not have emphasized this enough. We arranged for both English- and French-language play-by-play broadcasts. A Quebec restaurant group, La Cage aux Sports, was contracted to run the food-service operation. This was seen as a positive move by the French-speaking community, and La Cage had experience running the Québec Capitales' concessions. We arranged a decent contract with La Cage, which paid us a portion of its percentage ahead of time. They also spent over $150,000 up-fitting and setting up the concession operations. This was important, with money an issue by this time.

The baseball end was also coming together. Hal Lanier was hired to be our manager. Hal had been a major league manager with the Houston Astros and was named the National League's manager of the year in 1986. He had managed 16 seasons in independent baseball with great success. His name would add credibility for the skeptics who did not believe in the quality or professionalism of the independent game. We then signed Sébastien Boucher as our first player. Seb was originally from Gatineau and had been a seventh-round draft pick of the Seattle Mariners. He reached as high as Triple-A and for the previous five seasons had been one of the leading hitters with the Québec Capitales. He was bilingual. Those two names were important.

The Can-Am League was looking stronger for the 2015 season. In addition to Ottawa, the Sussex County (N.J.) Miners were added, bringing the league roster to six teams. Also, two foreign teams were scheduled to play in the league. Arrangements had been made to bring Cuba's national team and the all-star team from Japan's independent Shikoku Island League to participate for a month in the league. The Cuban team was a huge coup for the league. A Cuban team had not played in a professional league since 1960. The owners of the Shikoku Island League were covering the expense of bringing the Japanese team to North America.

Preseason sales of tickets were slow, but there was good news on several fronts. A three-year deal for naming rights was contracted at $150,000 a year with a national accounting firm. The beer rights for

There's a Bulldozer on Home Plate

exclusivity in the park went for $45,000. The flip side of the coin was our inability to sell sponsorship for our video board. An old dot-matrix scoreboard had been left over from the Triple-A years, but the Ottawa market needed more than that. A video board with graphics, live replays, and stats had to be part of the ballpark experience, and the cost was over $250,000. In Quebec when that franchise was started, a manual scoreboard was built for $25,000 with drop-in numbers and a goose that quacked. We portrayed that as "authentic" to go with the ancient ballpark. But I couldn't pull that trick in Ottawa. The hockey and the football teams were full of electronic gimmicks and the club needed to compete. I bit the bullet and ordered a large video board made in China. With no sponsorship, I hoped that down the road a firm might be convinced to be our partner with the board.

It was always hectic getting ready for any Opening Night, but the initial opening in Ottawa with a totally new staff and new problems was particularly scary. Our new GM was being overwhelmed and with two weeks to go, I took over many of his responsibilities. He was not prepared or equipped to deal with all the problems associated with opening a new franchise. The city had not completed all its work, and new slip-proof flooring at the main entrance had been incorrectly installed. The team offices were moved for two days as the city corrected the problem with less than a week to go. We had ordered a new ticketing system which was not totally installed until four hours before the opening. The video board was late from China and only installed two days before the opener. A hundred large and little things needed to be completed, but we opened on May 22 with almost everything in order. Some observers predicted that it would be a disaster, but our fans saw none of the problems. The Ottawa Champions were underway.

The Opening Night crowd, announced as 3,800, was not bad, and we remained hopeful. As the season went on, fans were saying good things about our operation and the team. Personally, I knew the operation was good. However, it was clear that not everything had "clicked." Crowds were in the 1,500 to 2,000 range, not the 2,500 we needed. Some good things had happened. The Cuba national team drew nearly 5,000 a game for three straight days. The attendance for the Japanese series was good, but rain canceled the final game. Our Canada Day game was rained out. This had been the biggest day financially for the Triple-A team. Sundays were our best days for attendance while in many minor league towns, it was the worst.

The season saw positives and negatives. Coverage from the English

16. Ottawa

media was marginal, while the French newspaper *Le Droit* gave the team good coverage. Concession per-caps were near $10, which was a good figure, and the food service received good reviews. The team finished in fifth place with a 46–50 record, and fans reacted positively to the players. The costume of our mascot, Champ, was worn by the former mascot portrayer of the Winnipeg Goldeyes, and the kids loved him. I would have given him a lifetime contract, but after two years, he was forced to quit. He was taking instruction to become a Ukrainian Catholic priest, and once he was ordained, the church would not allow him to continue. Ecclesiastical regulations on mascots were new to me.

Financially, the year was bad. The attendance for the year was 115,880, but financial statements showed a loss of over $700,000. Startup expenses were significant, and the club simply hadn't drawn enough spectators. Hope was still possible. The big games like the Cuban series had proven that people would come given the right circumstance, and I believed that word of mouth would help in the second year. Experience had shown that the third year was the key. If the team wasn't making a profit by then, it wasn't going to happen. I now knew what worked and what did not work in the market, and we had the fall and winter to prepare. I remained cautiously optimistic.

The optimism was not well-placed. In the second season the club drew 10,000 more fans. The team was better, finishing fourth, and the Champions got hot at the right time and made it to the finals in the playoffs. With the series tied 2–2, just one more win was needed to earn our name, the Champions. Yet, I found myself rooting desperately against the Champions. Perhaps, if the final game had been at home, I would have wanted our fans to experience the thrill of a championship. But the game was on the road in Rockland, and if the club won, I would have to buy rings for all the players and staff at a cost of over $15,000. Our bank account was empty. The Champions won, and I cheered appropriately, but my heart was not in it.

That year the losses fell to $400,000, and I began to take loans from the bank. I had always been undercapitalized and was now cutting corners everywhere. The visible operation did not change, but the operation was not running as smoothly as a quality operation should.

In the third season, attendance fell off slightly as the team finished 22 games out of first place. The handwriting on the wall was not good. The franchise was not going to make it. The three-year window for success was closing. By June, I stopped paying rent. The players needed to be paid rather than the city. In August a call came from the mayor's chief of staff to set up a meeting. The Champions' days seem numbered. At the meeting, I was prepared for the worst, but the meeting turned in a different direction. The chief of staff was adamant that the city of Ottawa wanted the team to stay and was prepared to lower the rent to $120,000 a year starting in 2018. This was amazing. That would save over $300,000 a season, and while this would not yet put the team in a profitable position, it would be close enough to give us hope of making a profit or at least making the losses manageable. We would have time to build our base of fans. It had taken seven years in Quebec before the organization consistently made money, and with a new lease, this now would be possible in Ottawa. The mayor's office would start working on a new lease immediately, and I could announce to the media that the team was returning for another year. The chief of staff asked us to wait on announcing the new lease until it was ready to be signed.

During all the involvement with Ottawa, the office in Durham continued to run the American Association, the Can-Am League, and the Burlington franchise. My role as commissioner still involved considerable time, but the two leagues were relatively stable. Dan Moushon had been supervising Burlington for 20 years and was one of the leaders in the Appalachian League. In 2017 the president of the Appy League announced he was retiring at the end of the 2018 season, and Dan Moushon was elected as the new president. With the rules of affiliated minor league baseball prohibiting any association with independent leagues, it would be necessary for Dan to leave his role as president of the Can-Am and American Association. Dan was ready for a new challenge, and the Appy League presidency was a position that ideally could give him more stability and job security. I was proud that Dan had been selected for the role.

However, the thought of running the two leagues without Dan was a non-starter, and the timing was right to make changes. I had been in independent ball for 25 years, and it was time for both leagues to consider new leadership. At the annual meetings in the fall, Dan and I announced that we both would be leaving at the end of the 2018 season. This would give time for each league to find new officers and make a smooth transition. I felt good about what had been accomplished. The Northern League started with six teams, hoping to survive, and now its successor league, the American Association, could be considered one of the top leagues in all of minor league sports. At the high point the Durham office supervised some 20 independent teams. The teams started in 1993 in ancient, creaky ballparks with few amenities.

16. Ottawa

Now, new stadiums had been built for almost every league member with suites, restaurants, and even swimming pools. These efforts had encouraged others to bring independent baseball to their communities. The fun remained, and winning mattered.

Back in Ottawa, the negotiations on the new lease were still secret and nothing had been released to the public. Six weeks after the first discussions on the lease I received another call from the mayor's chief of staff. He relayed that the mayor was concerned. The election for mayor of Ottawa was to be held in October 2018, and the mayor did not want to have the ballpark as an issue in the campaign. Could the Champions wait one more season for the new lease? This was tough. I had already announced the team was returning and had let league members know Ottawa was part of operations for 2018.

One of the regulations of the Can-Am League that had been put in place after the Allentown club pulled out of the league stipulated that each club would place a $200,000 letter of credit (LOC) with the league attorney to ensure operations. It was to be renewed every three years, and if a club shut down during that three-year period, the league would take the LOC. My $200,000 letter of credit for Ottawa was on file with the league attorney, and it would be lost if the franchise pulled out. I knew the club would have substantial losses in 2018, but these losses could be less than the LOC. With a new lease, the club would be much more attractive to potential new ownership. I might be able to recoup some of the losses. I had to stay.

By this time, I had let the GM go and was operating the club with a bare-bones staff. Attendance did go up slightly in 2018, even with a last-place finish. The team signed Éric Gagné for a one-game start on Labor Day. The former Dodger all-star was a hero in the province of Quebec, and for his appearance, the stadium was packed with nearly 8,000 fans. It was a tremendous success, and the deposit for the one day was well over $100,000. Days like that pointed to the potential of huge success for baseball in the city, but was Ottawa always to be a mirage?

The mayor won re-election easily in fall 2018, and it was time to push the city for the new lease. But it was not to be. The chief of staff informed me that the timing was not good, and by the time a lease could be presented to the council and go through the necessary bureaucratic machinations, it would be May with the season underway. The deadline was now 2020 for the new lease. The Champions were dead. The chief of staff was sincere in his efforts, but I had not pushed hard enough. I tried to accommodate the city when the concern should have been the club.

There's a Bulldozer on Home Plate

The problem was the same as the prior season. I had informed the league in the fall that the franchise would operate, and again I would lose the $200,000 letter of credit if it didn't. If I folded the team, losses would be less than they had been in previous seasons, which had been in the $400,000 range. However, I considered another less ethical route. If I did not pay the city rent for 2019, which was still around $400,000, I would have the chance to make it through the season and maybe find an owner. The first rent payment was not due until late May with the season underway. I had been late on rent payments before, and by the time it was evident that the rent was not coming, the season would be almost over. The politics of the city padlocking the ballpark in the middle of a season would not be a good visual. It was a necessary gamble.

The club needed operating capital to pay off 2018 debts and to pay staff through the winter months. I sold our house in Quebec. This did not please Michelle. For 20 years, we had spent much of our summers there, and it was as much our home as the house in Durham. The Quebec home sold quickly.

We made it through the season. Hal Lanier had not been rehired, and instead Sébastien Boucher was named manager. When Seb first agreed to come to Ottawa in 2015, he asked to be considered for manager when his playing career was over. He was 37 and it was time. Seb's salary requirements were less than Hal's. As usual, the team was mediocre and ended in fifth place, just out of the playoffs. The fans remained loyal, and the attendance was consistent with previous years, respectable, but never enough. It was August when the city's financial dogs began hounding the team for payment, but we were able to put them off until the season was over.

It would seem that all this was depressing: the financial losses, the pressure from the city, a team that could never win half its games. But no, I loved being owner of the Ottawa Champions. I loved being able to sit with Michelle in our seats at the stadium and cheer for the team. When I was only the commissioner, I could only root for the umpires with a quiet prayer that they wouldn't miss a call. But as owner, I could be a baseball fan once again. It was true I couldn't yell at the umpires—I still had my commissioner's hat nearby—but the Champions were my team and I could visibly show my emotions. I so wanted them to do well.

But it was not just the games that brought joy. I loved the experience of being at the stadium. It was great standing and listening to "Take Me Out to the Ball Game," for the ten thousandth time. I loved

16. Ottawa

helping pick out the music to play between innings—I'd tell the staff I wanted "happy" music—and it was a great pleasure to stand in line to buy a hot dog or burger just like every other fan. I could make certain the food was good and hot. Before the game I stood in front of the stadium and greeted the fans while also keeping an eye on the parking lot, hoping that the kids directing the cars would be overwhelmed and I would have to jump in to help. It rarely happened. I loved the silliness of the mascot and children lying on top of the dugout after the game trying to get an autograph.

The best time of a game was postgame when I could go down to the manager's office, grab a beer, and sit and talk about the game. It had started with Eddie Haas fifty years earlier, and over the years I would talk with Dirty Al or Scrap Iron or Hal Lanier or Singin' Ed and learn so much about baseball. Then as the stadium was closing up, I would go back to the office and get the game report on ticket and concession sales. This was my box score and the numbers mattered. And finally, always after 11 p.m. unless extra innings intruded, I drove to the apartment where Michelle would have a glass of wine waiting with cheese and crackers. We would talk and it was always the best way to end the evening. And if I was lucky and the schedule cooperated, I would repeat everything the next night and the following night. I loved being owner of the Ottawa Champions.

I had worked too hard on keeping baseball in Ottawa to simply walk away, and the mayor's office wanted to keep baseball. The new lease that had been worked on for the last two years was now available to a new owner if the old rent was paid. I found one local businessman who was willing to pay the back rent plus $100,000 for the inventory and goodwill. That would be enough to pay our final bills. Sam Katz of Winnipeg was ready to take over the lease, paying back rent, but I would get nothing. It was up to the city to make that decision and Sam Katz was chosen. He requested the 2020 season off to prepare for a season with no lingering baggage. The city consented, and then padlocked the ballpark with the remaining office supplies and equipment. I had arranged for the baseball uniforms and baseball equipment to be given to a local school but that was not allowed by city personnel. Everything the Champions had acquired was now property of the city of Ottawa.

I look back on five years in Ottawa without much regret. I lost over $2 million, which I do regret, and it changed my personal financial situation. In terms of baseball, it was a great experience. I worked hard,

There's a Bulldozer on Home Plate

but it just didn't come together. I had success in other markets using the same formula, but it may have been just time for me to find a little humility. I looked for reasons, but was I just looking for excuses? Many said that Ottawa was just not a baseball town. I don't believe it. Too many good fans supported us. We just needed a few more.

It is difficult to single out one specific factor that caused failure. I can point out the demise of newspapers. The *Ottawa Citizen* and the *Ottawa Sun* were losing their reach when the team arrived. In past operations, I needed the press to get the word out on the team. Print newspapers were always the one voice that everyone in a community looked to. The internet was changing that. In the first season, the *Citizen* had a reporter at almost every game, but by the end, the *Sun* and the *Citizen* had merged and few reporters in the English media ever came to games. The sports department was down to three writers with hockey and football always having daily coverage. Social media worked well, but that didn't cover the entire community. I was always surprised that many locals did not know the team even existed. The Champions came into the market with hockey dominating and with football getting the honeymoon effect. The Champions were at best an also-ran. But Ottawa was a market of 1.2 million, enough population that the franchise should have been profitable. Perhaps with massive spending on advertising, it might have made a difference, but I always operated with little funding to spare.

The franchise in Madison always came to mind when I replayed Ottawa. Madison had all the elements that were needed for a successful franchise, yet it failed. But the very next season, a new operator arrived in a new league with great success. He found the key. I believed Ottawa could enjoy great success in baseball, but someone needed to find the right key. I wish I had been the one to open the lock, but it was not to be.

By October, I was back in North Carolina. I was no longer a commissioner and no longer had ties to independent baseball. I was not looking to retire, but it was time to step back. I still had the Burlington team in the Appalachian League that could cover my need for a baseball fix. For 35 years, I had owned the team but always left it up to Dan Moushon to supervise. Now that he was president of the Appalachian League, it was time to be involved. A quality staff handled operations, and I was ready to enjoy the games as owner.

In December I attended the Winter Meetings for the first time in years. As commissioner of an independent league, I had not been

16. Ottawa

Burlington, North Carolina. The ballpark in Burlington was originally located in Danville, Virginia, as home of the Danville Leafs in the Carolina League. When Danville folded in 1958, the city of Burlington bought the Danville park for $5000 and moved it piece by piece to Burlington. It became home for Burlington Baseball in the Carolina League in 1960. That franchise folded after the 1971 season and did not return until 1986 when the Cleveland Indians placed an Appalachian League team in the city. That franchise remained for 35 years until the MLB contracted the minors in 2020.

welcomed, and it was good to see old friends that I had lost contact with over the years. Minor League Baseball was now a much larger enterprise, and it was interesting to see how much the organization had grown. At the meetings, reports circulated that Major League Baseball was planning to make significant cuts to the minor leagues. Rumors had started in the summer, and now the rumors were real. Lawyers had been hired, Members of Congress alerted, and the minors appeared ready to face Big Brother head on. It was a bit of déjà vu all over again. Thirty years earlier, the majors had come to dismantle the minors, and out of that threat, the independent leagues started.

For me, the most disturbing information being circulated was that the Appalachian League was one of the leagues on the chopping block. The majors effectively owned the Appy League and it would be an easy league to eliminate. In January, Dan Moushon and I met with our U.S. congressman to get political support. The city of Burlington appeared ready to take legal action to protect the city's investment of over a million dollars in the last few years in the Burlington ballpark. At the same time, I was making several trips a week to Burlington to become better acquainted with the operation.

Then in early February, everything changed. The GM and assistant GM both announced they were leaving the club for other jobs. With the threat from MLB, they were worried about the future of the Burlington team. Both felt they had to make a move. I was left with no employees and a season starting in four months. In the past, I might have viewed this as a challenge. I had experienced more difficult situations in the past and had succeeded. Now, I was simply panicked. I had just come from a challenging situation in Ottawa in a major market and had made it through five years. Now, the thought of running an operation for one year in a city of 50,000 was overwhelming. I realized I had no desire to set up another team. I hated my thinking, but the message was clear. My time was over.

    I called Dan Moushon. Could he find new ownership on such short notice? Within a week, a former Burlington GM was ready to buy, even with MLB's plan for the league hanging over the franchise's head. The purchase price was only $150,000, but it did not matter. I had to leave. One week after I signed the sales agreement, the Covid-19 pandemic became a major factor, but the new owner was willing to continue with the deal. The Durham Bulls' stockholders who had invested 40 years earlier received one final check from an investment that had netted them nearly a hundred times the original investment. And I was now totally out of baseball.

Epilogue

The year 2020 was my first without baseball. It also was the year of Covid-19, and no baseball was played in any minor leagues. A few independent teams attempted an abbreviated schedule. My sense of loss was muted as everyone experienced a vacuum in the lives they had lived. Michelle and I hunkered down in Durham but kept up with our kids whose lives we followed from afar. Baby boys had been born in both households in the previous two years, and the pleasure of grandparenting arrived. Hoffman was in Quebec City doing consulting work. He still was a fan of Les Capitales and had ties to the American Association as he edited its media guide each year. Claire was married and in St. Louis, teaching and involved in social work in the city. She no longer had an aversion to baseball and had become a Cardinals fan. Once a year, she would remember her roots and take a group of friends across the Mississippi River to Sauget, Illinois, to see a Gateway Grizzlies game in the independent Frontier League. Her friends were always amazed that she was comfortable in this strange environment of mascots, hamburgers served in Krispy Kreme donuts, and people cheering for players they had never heard of. It was an Americana many had never seen, and it pleased me when she relayed stories of these trips.

Minor league baseball had given me so much over the years. It had given me a career, a family, and good friends. I had come to know and appreciate the United States and Canada as I searched for ballparks in 50 states and nine Canadian provinces. I discovered the fascinating cities of Savannah, Quebec, Butte, Duluth, and others that normally I would never have seen.

One of the last states I visited was Alaska when my family gave me a trip to attend the Midnight Sun Game in Fairbanks. The legendary game was played on the longest day of the year when there was no need for lights. Starting around 10:30, the game was interrupted at midnight as the crowd sang the Alaska state anthem. The team was the Fairbanks Goldpanners, a club in the summer collegiate Alaska Baseball League.

There's a Bulldozer on Home Plate

Chatting with the GM of the team, I asked when the lights were normally turned on. He told me that the lights no longer worked and had not been needed or turned on in thirty years.

Baseball had given me the opportunity to work with great people, individuals who had the same passion for the game as I did. I could start listing names, but it would be pages long and I would certainly leave someone out. I had the good fortune to work with baseball people with names like Scraps and Singin' Ed, and Dirty Al and T-Bone. How many adult jobs have so many interesting people with so many unique names?

The baseball world was changing. The Burlington team and the Appy League survived. Dan Moushon started working with MLB, and plans were developed for the Appy League to become a summer college wood bat league with an affiliation with the majors. Because of Covid, no affiliated minor-league baseball was being played in 2020, but the Appy League, through the new arrangements with MLB, was in a good position for long-term survival. In 2021, the first season back, fans responded well to the new college structure, and the league had a successful year. Burlington still had baseball, and the new owner had an asset that could be valuable.

As the Covid-19 pandemic expanded, Minor League Baseball no longer had the will to fight the majors. The political efforts directed toward Washington fell off the radar of Members of Congress as the coronavirus took center stage. The fight was dead to save the 42 teams that the majors proposed to cut. Now minor league clubs were fighting each other to be one of the 120 that would be kept. MLB demands were acquiesced to immediately. The minor league office in St. Petersburg was dismantled and 60 employees were let go. The minors were now run by a gaggle of lawyers in New York City. It was not pretty.

The major leagues did make efforts to find homes and help the 42 clubs they had cut. The Pioneer League became an independent league with limited support from MLB. Some questioned whether the Pioneer League markets were large enough to support an independent operation, but the league had few options. Other former affiliated teams joined various college leagues and a few joined the existing independent leagues. The independent leagues were invited to come under the major league umbrella with a new designation, "partner leagues." MLB made strong assurances on the help they could give the independents, but other than gaining a major league label, it was difficult to see many advantages. As a first move, MLB took three of the best independent franchises. From

16. Epilogue

the American Association, the St. Paul Saints departed and became the Triple-A affiliate of the Minnesota Twins. In the Atlantic League, Sugar Land left and became the Triple-A affiliate of the Houston Astros, while the Somerset Patriots became the Double-A affiliate of the New York Yankees. These moves significantly weakened their former leagues.

Dan Moushon, whose judgment I always trust, believes that ultimately these changes will give more stability to minor league baseball and the result will be good. I hope Dan is right but I have considerable doubt. I do not trust MLB nor do I believe it has the best interests of baseball in its sights. It says it will help player development, yet many major league teams want more farm teams. Big-league teams are now limited to four affiliated teams, and the draft has been reduced to twenty rounds. At one point the draft was 50 or more rounds, and the number of good major leaguers who came from the lower rounds was significant. MLB told the minor leagues that a reconfiguration of the leagues was necessary because excessive travel is a burden on the players, yet the new league boundaries are byzantine. It complains about facilities and asks cities to make significant improvements, yet its actions in deleting 42 franchises make it doubtful that city governments will ever want to invest in ballparks again when MLB is able to eliminate the hometown team on a whim.

One of the most worrisome aspects of MLB taking over the minors is that no one in the offices in New York has ever worked in the minors. There is no love, no passion, no knowledge of the bush leagues. No one will be there to speak for the smaller cities. No one in the office knows or appreciates the history and traditions.

The commissioner is a lawyer, and the offices are populated with lawyers who have little feel for the game. Few have even seen a minor league game. They looked at the minor leagues and decided that because they have degrees which indicate they must be smart, they now can take over the minors and do a better job. They are just playing Monopoly. The purpose is to control properties and hotels—in this case, leagues and teams—and like children, they will grow tired of the game and when their efforts have failed, they will turn to other games and the minors will wither.

But there is always hope, because baseball has always been able to survive those who run it. And when the current plan has changed and cities are left without baseball, someone will see an empty ballpark and remember how much fun it was when a team played there. And maybe a dream will start, and the thought will emerge that it should happen again. And others will join in the dream and think that baseball should start in their city. Players will hear about it and want to pursue their dreams of playing professional baseball. Fans will become excited, and one summer's evening, thousands will show up, and the joy that was lost will return to once empty fields. It is always good to have a dream.

conversation between commissioner and league president
Northern League, 1997

"We've got a problem with two of our managers."
"What's the problem?"
"Both managers were thrown out of the game between Fargo and St. Paul last night."
"So what's the problem? Fine them $50 and move on."
"Well, the problem is they returned to the field of play later in the game."
"That's serious. They knew they shouldn't be doing that."
"It's something different. They were just having fun. They had put on the Sumo suits for the wrestling promotion between innings and actually took part in the wrestling match. The crowd loved it."
"Who won?"
"The Fargo manager."
"Can you really tell who is in those costumes when they're on the field?"
"Not really, but the umpires figured it out and thought the managers were trying to show them up."
"OK, double the fine and tell the umpires the league has a new rule that managers are not allowed on the field in Sumo suits."

Appendix:
Careers in Independent Baseball (1993–2019)

When the Northern League was formed in 1993, the most-asked question was where players would come from. How can a whole league be filled with rejects? These players have been told they aren't good enough, that their baseball career is over. Yet many of these athletes still have the dream and they come to the independent leagues. Some may play only a season, but others come back year after year. There is a saying in baseball that "players leave when you rip the uniform off their backs." The game is addictive, and it is tough to let go. Fans may yell at a player, "Get a real job!," but this is a real job for them. Why do you have to give up something you love?

In the first year of the Northern League, when I asked the Thunder Bay manager how many of his players would want to come back, and he told me all of them, I was shocked. But now, looking at the records of the players in the league, at least four have played over 15 seasons, and as many as 63 have played for ten years or more. They certainly aren't doing it for the money. When the most any player will make at tops is around $3,000 a month for four months, and many will make around $2,000 monthly, this is certainly not going to make them rich. For some of the Latino players, it is a better job than they can get in their home country, but just as many American players with college degrees are playing until age and skills betray them.

One player who was sold to a major league club was asked why he had continued in independent ball. His response: "I thought about it every day, honestly. What kept me coming back to the ballpark was being around your teammates and your coaches and having fun in the clubhouse. The thing you realize when you go to independent baseball

Appendix

is how much you're doing this not for the money or the dream, (but) how much fun you have playing it. Since it's such an authentic type of baseball, independent baseball, meaning that this is the only team that matters, it's really just putting wins and losses up in the columns. You don't have to worry about moving through an organization. You kind of go back to the basics and you realize you're doing this to have fun."

Most of the players who ended up making a "career" in the independent leagues become baseball "lifers." Baseball is their life. In the off-season they may play winter ball or they may be part of baseball complexes in their home city where they teach young aspiring players. I like to look at the *Baseball America Directory* when it comes out each spring and try to count the number of independent alumni who are still in the game. Many of them have gone back to affiliated baseball as managers and coaches. Quite a few are on big-league coaching staffs. I see the names of scouts and college coaches. Some are in major league front offices, and at least one is an assistant major league GM. Some players have gone back to coaching their high school teams, and even those who do not make their living at baseball are Little League and youth coaches. One has coached at the Little League World Series.

It is not just the players in independent baseball who have continued in the game. At least six umpires have made the big leagues, and a good number of front-office personnel are now working in major league front offices. Bob Freitas once confided to me that baseball was like a cancer. It was all-consuming and there was little protection. When he first told me that, I didn't understand. After 50 years, I now do. I never was able to leave the game and kept looking for new cities, new chances to spread the gospel. It is difficult to understand why I believed that every city should have a team, but I did. It was always a loss when one didn't make it, but there was pride in those that have remained and succeeded.

Following are lists of position players and pitchers with 10 years or more of independent ball under their belts, as well as a list of managers who have put in at least 14 years.

Careers in Independent Baseball (1993–2019)

Ten or More Seasons in Independent Baseball, Hitters (32)

Name	Yrs.	Leagues	Seasons
Jorge Alvarez	16	Tx-LA/Central, Atlantic, Am. Assn.	1995–97, 1999–2010, 2012
Eddie Lantigua	16	Northern, Northeast/Can-Am	1994–2010, 2012
Fehlandt Lentini	14	Front., North., Gold., AA, Atl., Pac. Assn.	2004–17
Aharon Eggleston	13	Northern, Atlantic, AA	2005–17
Willis Otanez	13	Atlantic	2002–13, 2015
Vic Davilla	12	Can-Am, Northeast, Am. Assn.	1994–2005
Sandy DeLeon	12	Front., Atl., Golden, Can-Am, United	2000–07, 09–11, 13
Blake Gailen	12	S. Coast, Atlantic, AA, Golden	2007–18
Craig Maddox	12	Can-Am, Northern, Atlantic, AA	2008–19
Josh Patton	12	Northern, American Association	1997–2008
Larry Bethea	11	Atlantic, Northeast, Northern, AA, TX-LA, SE, Central, Can-Am, United	1998–2008
Ken Craddox	11	Northern, Frontier, Northeast, Southeast	1993–2003
Bryant Nelson	11	Atlantic, Can-Am	2006–16
Ed Gerald	11	Prairie, Northern, Central, NE/Can-Am	1995–2005
Vic Gutierrez	11	Atlantic	2001–02, 2004–05, 2007–13
Max Poulin	11	Tx/LA, Northern, AA, Gold., Can-Am	1998, 2001–09, 2014
Luis Rodriguez	11	Atlantic, Can-Am	2004–05, 2007–15
Brad Straus	11	Frontier, Prairie, Atlantic	1994–96, 2000–07
Reg. Abercrombie	10	American Association	2010–19
Luis Alen	10	Northern, AA, Atlantic, Can-Am	2007, 2010–18
Elio Ayala	10	Canadian, Atl., North., Front., Can-Am	2003–12
Sébastien Boucher	10	Can-Am	2009–18
Steve Brown	10	Golden, Nor. American, Can-Am	2010–19
Angel Espada	10	Atlantic	1998–2007

Appendix

Name	Yrs.	Leagues	Seasons
Lew Ford	10	Atlantic	2009, 2011–19
Norm Hutchins	10	NE, Golden, Can-Am, Atl., AA	2002–09, 2011–12
Palmer Karr	10	Central, United, Can-Am, Am. Assoc.	2005–14
Alex Llanos	10	Atlantic, Central, Northern, AA	2000–09
Luis Lopez	10	Northern, AA, Can-Am, Atlantic	1995, 2006–14
Alex Nunez	10	Can-Am, AA, Atlantic	2005, 2007–12, 2014–16
Ross Peeples	10	Atlantic	2005–14
Chris Van Rossum	10	Northern, Atl., Southeast, Golden	2000–01, 2003–10

Ten or More Seasons in Independent Baseball, Pitchers (30)

Name	Yrs.	Leagues	Seasons
Isaac Pavlik	15	Northeast/Can-Am	2004–17, 2019
Kris Regas	15	Frontier, AA, Atlantic, Can-Am	2002–09, 2011–17
John Brownell	13	Atlantic, Frontier, Northern, AA	2007–19
Karl Gélinas	14	Can-Am	2007–19, 2021
Ryan Harris	13	Western, T-L, Cent., United, Atl., AA, Northern, North American	1998–2009, 2011
Greg Bicknell	12	TL, Northern, Western, AA, Golden	1995–2001, 2004–08
Joe Gannon	12	NE/Can-Am, Atl., Canadian, AA	2002–09, 2011–14
Ricardo Gomez	12	South Coast, Atlantic	2007–12, 2014–19
Ned Darley	11	Western, Atlantic, AA, Northern	1995, 1997–98, 2000–01, 03–08
Tim Cain	11	Northern, Atlantic	1994, 1998–2007
Rich Hyde	11	Northern	1994, 1996–2005
Eric Moran	11	Northern, TX-LA, Southeast, United	1993–2002, 2009
Matt Schweitzer	11	Frontier, Northern, Atlantic	2000–10
Matt Smith	11	Atlantic, Northern, Northeast	1999–2003, 2006–11
Jeff Bittiger	10	Northern	1993–2002

Careers in Independent Baseball (1993–2019)

Name	Yrs.	Leagues	Seasons
Pedro Flores	10	Tex-LA, Central, Atlantic, AA	2000–08, 2011
Andy High	10	Northeast, Atlantic	1996–2001, 2003–06
John Kelly	10	Northeast, Can-Am	1999, 2003–11
Trevor Marcotte	10	NE, Northern, Can-Am, Cent., AA, Atl.	2001–08, 2010–11
Kevin McGovern	10	Frontier, Pecos, American Assn.	2010–2021
Linc Mikkelsen	10	Northern, N. Central, Prairie, Atl.	1993–94, 1996, 2001–07
Eric Montoya	10	Front., TL, Cent., Atl., North., Un., AA	2000–08, 2010
Jason Moody	10	Atl., Front., United, Central, AA, N. Am.	1999–2003, 2006–07, 2010–12
Ben Moore	10	Northern, AA, Can-Am, Atlantic	2005–2014
Ross Peeples	10	Atlantic	2005–14
Matt Pike	10	NE, Northern, AA, Can-Am, Atlantic	2002–03, 2005–12
Mike "Texas" Smith	10	Tex-LA, Central, Atlantic, United	1995, 1998–2006
Kyle Ruwe	10	Northern, AA, Atlantic	2005–14
Richard Salazar	10	American Association, Can-Am	2008–17
T. J. Stanton	10	Northern, Amer. Assoc., Can-Am	2004, 2006–14

Independent Managers with at Least 14 Years of Service (1993–2019)

Name	Yrs.	Leagues	Seasons
Doug Simunic	25	Northern, Am. Assoc.	1993–2017
Greg Tagert	25	Frontier, Prairie, Northern, Am. Assoc.	1995–2019
Andy McCauley	22	Frontier, Northeast, Northern, Am. Assoc.	1998–2019
George Tsamis	21	Northeast, Northern, Am. Assoc.	1999–2019
Butch Hobson	21	Atlantic, Can-Am, Am. Assoc.	1995, 2000–19
Hal Lanier	20	Northern, Am. Assoc., Frontier, Can-Am.	1996–2018
Joe Calfapietra	20	Northeast, Northern, Can-Am, Am. Assoc.	2000–19
Jamie Keefe	17	Frontier, Can-Am, Atlantic	2001–19

Appendix

Name	Yrs.	Leagues	Seasons
Al Gallagher	17	Lone Star, Western, Northern, Am. Assoc., United, North Am.	1977, 1995–2012
Doc Edwards	16	Northeast, Frontier, Northern, Atlantic, United, North Am.	1995–2012
Wayne Krenchicki	16	Tex.-La., Northern, Atlantic, Frontier	1995–2010
Ed Nottle	16	Northern, Am. Assoc., Northeast, Can-Am	1993–2008
Dan Shwam	16	Northern, Northeast, Frontier, Central, Can-Am, United	1993–2009
Mike Pinto	15	Northern, Am. Assoc., Frontier	2005–2019
Rick Forney	14	Northern, Am. Assoc.	2006–2019
Jeff Isom	14	Frontier, Northern	2000–2006, 2013–19
Fran Riordan	14	Frontier	2000–2002, 2004–14

Index

Aaron, Hank 18, 21, 27, 38, 54
Aaron, Tommie (T-Bone) 21, 38–41
Aces 141–142
Alaska Goldpanners 126
Alexandria, Virginia 42
All-America Baseball News 57, 124
Allentown, Pennsylvania, Ambassadors 141, 142, 157
Amarillo, Texas 36, 111, 143
American Association 92, 108, 145, 147, 156, 163
American Hockey League (AHL) 76, 77
American Legion 91, 93, 116
American Tobacco Company 49, 72, 75
Anderson, South Carolina 27, 28, 29, 30, 31, 32, 127
Anderson Mets 27, 28, 29, 30
Appalachian League 57, 58, 110, 111, 143, 156, 160, 161, 163
Asheville, North Carolina Tourists 57, 62
Athens, Georgia 8
Atlanta, Georgia 9, 15
Atlanta Braves 9–11, 15, 18, 20–22, 24, 26, 31, 36, 38, 39, 41, 44, 45, 50, 52, 54, 57, 58, 95, 101, 114
Atlantic Coast Conference (ACC) 65, 78
Atlantic Coast League 113
Atlantic League 141, 165

Baker, Frank "Home Run" 62
Baker, Gene 40
Ballpark Corner 53, 127
Baltimore, Maryland 4, 6
Baltimore Orioles 4, 5, 6, 9, 15, 63, 66
Baseball America 57, 68, 75, 87, 104, 123–130
Baseball Hall of Fame 61
Baseball Weekly 129
The Battered Bastards of Baseball 24

Beauchamp, Kash 106
Belmonte, Nick 103, 105
Bender, Chief 62
Berger, Phil 84, 85
Bickel, Bud 110
Big South League 114
Birmingham, Alabama 44
Bittiger, Jeff 104
Bock, Jeff 57
Bock, Pete 51, 52, 53, 54, 55, 56, 67, 76, 77, 78, 81, 83
Borders, Ila 4, 118, 120, 121
Boston, Massachusetts "Miracle Braves" 62, 130
Boucher, Sébastien 153, 158
Bouton, Jim 24
Boyd, Dennis "Oil Can" 4
The Boys of Summer 59
Bramham, Judge William 62
Bresnahan, Roger 63
Brissie, Lou 11
Brockton, Massachusetts 141, 144, 146
Brophy, John 83
Bryant, John 111
Bryant, Steve 70
Buffalo, New York 86
Buffett, Jimmy 103
Bull Durham (movie) 46, 67, 68, 69
Bull Durham Smoking Tobacco 47, 62
Burlington, North Carolina 57, 58, 161
Burlington Indians/Royals 75, 143, 153, 160, 163
Butte, Montana Copper Kings 57

La Cage aux Sports 153
Can-Am League 142, 143, 147, 148, 149, 150, 156, 157
Canseco, Jose 65
Carbo, Bernie 35
Carolina Hurricanes 80

Index

Carolina League 9, 41, 42, 44, 45, 50, 57, 58, 65, 70, 104, 161
Carolina Theatre 68
Carty, Rico 11
Central League 143, 145
Chapel Hill, North Carolina 49
USS *Charles P. Cecil* (DD-835) 8
Charleston, West Virginia 37
Chase, Dave 127
Chen, Horn 143
Chesterfield cigarettes 49
Chicago White Sox 98, 99
Clark, Will 65
Clemson University 27
Cleveland Indians 11, 58, 99, 161
Coastal Plain League 42
Cobb, Ty 62, 63
Collins, Eddie 62
Collins, Jim 31
Colombia 81
Columbus, Georgia 20, 70, 71
Columbus, Ohio 37, 57
Conroy, Pat 17
Costner, Kevin 66, 69
Côté, Jean-François "Jeff" 130, 131, 132
Courtney, Clint "Scrap Iron" 15–18, 21, 39, 119, 159
Courtney, Dorothy 17
Cuban National Team 153, 154

Dalton, Harry 6
Devereaux Meadow 70
Dionne, Stephane 133
"Dirty Al" *see* Gallagher, Al
Disco Demolition Night 98
Dorton Arena 76, 78, 80, 82, 83, 84
Duke University 49, 55, 63, 72, 78, 82
Duluth, Minnesota 87, 88, 89, 96, 97, 98, 111
Duluth Dukes 104, 117, 134, 140
Dunn, Jack 63
Durham, Leon "Bull" 4, 106, 113
Durham, North Carolina 18, 36, 38, 44–51, 55, 56, 61, 64, 65, 66, 69–75, 126, 127, 129, 135, 143, 156
Durham Athletic Park (DAP) 45, 46, 54, 56, 65, 66, 71, 72, 74
Durham Bulls 15, 45, 46, 49, 50, 52–57, 61–66, 70, 71, 72, 73, 75, 76, 83, 97, 98, 103, 119, 124, 125, 145, 151, 162

East Coast Hockey League (ECHL) 76, 77, 81, 82, 84, 86, 143

Eastern League 45, 57, 130, 141, 148, 150, 152
Eight Men Out 66
Elmira, New York 144
Engel, Bruce 95, 105

Fairchild Park 58
Fargo, North Dakota 92, 93, 115
Fargo-Moorhead RedHawks 116, 140, 145
Fatsis, Stefan 106
Fayetteville, North Carolina 79
Federal League 63
Fewster, Chick 63
Fichman, Mal 96, 104
Fine, Judge Julius 39, 40
Fisk, Carlton 35
Ft. Worth, Texas 145
Fox, Charlie 119
Fox, Marshall 9, 94, 95
Freehan, Bill 89
Freitas, Bob 23, 24, 25, 26, 42, 96, 102, 103, 124, 125, 168
Frenchville, Maine 132
Frontier League 110, 111, 163

Gagné, Éric 138, 139, 157
Gallagher, Al "Dirty Al" 18, 44, 52, 56, 57, 118, 119, 120, 132, 159
Gammons, Peter 128
Garagiola, Joe 34
Gary, Indiana 141, 145
Gastonia, North Carolina 44
Gateway Grizzlies 163
Gatineau, Quebec 153
George, Phyllis 11
Golden State League 113
Goldklang, Marv 95, 98, 99, 100, 105, 120, 133
Good Enough to Dream 59
Goodman, Jim 73, 74, 75
Gorman, Lou 6
Grayson Stadium 11, 12, 20
Great Central League 101, 112, 113
Greensboro, North Carolina 4–5, 7, 15, 16, 58, 84
Greensboro Monarchs 84
Greensboro Patriots 4, 5
Greensboro Yankees, G-Yanks 4, 5
Guerrero, Pedro 4, 106
Guimond, Michelle 59–61; *see also* Wolff, Michelle

Index

Haas, Eddie 15, 39
Hagerstown, Maryland 58
Hampton Roads 77
Hartford Whalers 80
Hawaii Islanders 76
Helyar, Joe 50
Henderson, Al 12
Hitchcock, Billy 16
HOK architecture 72
Holland, Marcus 39
Horton, Willie 89
Houston Colt .45s 16

International League 33, 36, 37, 38, 63, 142

Jackson, Sonny 38
Jacksonville, Florida 32, 33, 35
Jacksonville Express 32
Jacksonville Suns 32, 34, 35
Japanese team *see* Shikoku Island
Johns Hopkins University 6, 22, 125
Johnson, Lloyd 128
Johnson, Lyndon 6, 7
Johnson, Walter "Big Train" 62, 63
Joliet, Illinois 141

Kahn, Roger 59
Kansas City, Kansas 140, 145
Kansas City Royals 33, 34
Katz, Sam 93, 115, 159
Kemp, David 91, 105
Kinston, North Carolina 41, 42, 43
Kleinendorst, Kurt 83

Lanier, Hal 153, 158, 159
Lantigua, Eddie 138, 139
Laplante, Michel 132, 133, 135, 139
Laredo, Texas 145
Lee, Bill 111
Leip, Tom 105
Lethbridge Dodgers 126
Lewis and Clark Park 107
Liggett and Myers Tobacco 49
Ligtenberg, Kerry 114
Lincoln, Nebraska 118, 141, 145
Little Falls, New York 144
Lone Star League 86, 103
Los Angeles Dodgers 138, 157
Lucky Strike cigarettes 49
Lunch at the Five and Ten 7
Lunsford, Buford 28, 29, 30, 31

Mack, Connie 62, 63, 64
Macon, Georgia 44, 45
Macon Peaches 44
Madison, Wisconsin 115, 116, 118, 132, 160
Madison Black Wolf 116, 118, 120, 132, 133
Making My Pitch 120
May, Ricky 95, 97, 98, 105, 108
Mayo Field 94
Mays, Willie 30, 31
Mazzilli, Lee 31
McClain, Denny 89
McKeon, Jack 58
McPhail, Andy 106
Meadows, Lee "Spec" 64
Memorial Stadium, Baltimore 6
Memorial Stadium, Greensboro 5, 16
Metrodome 92, 106
Miami Miracle 98
Midway Stadium 93, 106, 108
Midwest League 116
Miller, Bill 53
Mills, Jim 41, 42, 51
Minneapolis, Minnesota 88, 92, 93
Minnesota Twins 92, 106, 163
Minoso, Minnie 4
Mitchell, Kevin 114
Montclair, New Jersey 141
Montréal, Quebec 130, 148
Montréal Expos 130, 134, 136, 138
Moorhead, Minnesota 116
Morris, Jack 4
Morris, Ron 52
Mount, Bonnie 60, 68, 69
Mount, Lillard 51, 60, 68, 108, 126
Mount, Thom 50, 51, 52, 54, 66, 68
Moushon, Dan 131, 141, 143, 144, 156, 160, 161, 162, 164, 165
Murdock Center, Butner, North Carolina 60
Murnane Field 59
Murray, Bill 103
The Music Man 1

Nashville, Tennessee 57
National Association of Professional Baseball 23, 45, 110, 130
National Hockey League (NHL) 76, 79, 81, 83, 86, 131
New Jersey Jackals 141
New York Mets 30, 31
New York-Pennsylvania League 57

Index

Newport, Rhode Island 7, 8
North American Soccer League 26
North Atlantic League 113
North Carolina A&T University 7
North Carolina Central University 49
North Carolina State University 49, 78, 80
North Central League 111, 112, 113
North Dakota State University 116
Northeast League 113, 122, 131, 134, 140, 144, 146
Northern League 4, 87, 88, 90, 93, 97, 99, 101, 102, 103, 107, 108, 110, 115, 118, 120, 122, 130, 140, 144, 147, 156, 167
Northwest League 23, 24, 25, 26, 42, 43, 105, 106
Nottle, Ed "Singin' Ed" 104, 121, 146, 159

Oklahoma City University 134
Orion Pictures 66
Ornest, Harry 43
Ornest, Ruthie 43
Ottawa, Ontario 142, 143, 147, 149–160, 162
Ottawa Champions 152, 154, 155, 157, 158, 159
Ottawa Redblacks 152
Ottawa Senators 152

Pacific Coast League 24
Paris, France 8
Parker Field 36
Pasco, Ed 31
Patkin, Max 5, 67
Pereira, Bill 95, 96, 105, 121
Pereira, Cord 97
Peters, Frank "The Flake" 24
Pettaway, "Big" Ike 18
Philadelphia Athletics 62
Pierce, Byron 111
Pioneer League 57, 102, 164
Pittsfield, Massachusetts 44
Pluto, Terry 128
Portland, Oregon 24, 25, 26, 86
Portland Beavers 24
Portland Mavericks 24
Price, Jackie 5
Provincial League 130
USS *Puget Sound* (AD-380) 8
Pulaski, Virginia 57

Quebec City, Quebec 81, 118, 122, 130–139, 144, 148, 154, 158, 163

Québec Capitales (Les Capitales) 133, 135, 141, 143, 147, 151, 153, 163
Québec Nordiques 131
Quisenberry, Dan 34

Raleigh, North Carolina 49, 69, 70, 71, 74, 75, 78, 79, 81, 82
Raleigh IceCaps 77–86, 151
Rickey, Branch 10, 24
Richmond, Virginia 18, 21, 36, 37, 38, 39, 41, 63
Richmond Braves 37, 39, 40, 41
Robbins, Tim 66
Robinson, Eddie 9
Robinson, Jackie 7
Rochester, Minnesota 92, 93, 100, 101, 104, 106, 107, 115, 117
Rocky Mount, North Carolina Pines 45, 58, 96, 102
Rousakis, John 11
Russell, Bing 24
Ruth, Babe 27
Ryan, Nolan 149

St. Cloud, Minnesota 92, 93, 111
St. Joseph, Missouri 145
St. Louis Browns 16, 99
St. Paul, Minnesota 88, 92, 93, 99, 100, 102, 108
St. Paul Saints 92, 106, 107, 108, 114, 120, 122, 133, 134, 145, 165
Salt Lake City, Utah, Trappers 86, 102, 103, 104
San Francisco Giants 119
San Jose Bees 95
Sanders, Charles 95, 101, 104, 105
Sarandon, Susan 66
Sauget, Illinois 163
Sauter, Doug 83
Savannah, Georgia 9–12, 14, 15, 17, 18, 36, 39, 40, 43, 47–48
Savannah Braves 9, 18, 20, 24, 35, 44
Savannah Beach, Georgia 19, 23, 24, 26, 29, 35
Schaumburg, Illinois 90, 120, 141
Schley, Van 50, 59, 102, 105, 145, 146
Schwam, Dan 104, 108
Scott, George 112
Scranton, Pennsylvania 36
"Scraps," "Scrap Iron" *see* Courtney, Clint
Scripture, Billy 33–35
Season of the Owl 52

Index

Shelby, North Carolina 29
Shelton, Ron 66, 67, 69
Shikoku Island League 153, 154
Shreveport, Louisiana 11
Shuttleworth, Paul "Red" 119
Simpson, Allan 126, 127, 128, 129
Simunic, Doug 104
Sioux City, Iowa 1, 2, 93, 100, 101, 104, 106, 107, 140
Sioux City Explorers 121, 145
Sioux Falls, South Dakota 1, 2, 4, 87, 91, 100, 140
Sioux Falls Canaries 4, 104, 113, 145
Sioux Falls Stadium 91
South Atlantic League (Sally League) 57, 58
Southern League 32, 39, 44, 45, 71
The Sporting News 15, 87, 124, 125, 128
Staab, Matt 91, 100
Le Stade de Québec 130, 131, 137
Staub, Rusty 16
Stavernos, Harry 94, 95, 100, 105, 120
Strawberry, Darryl 4, 121
Superior, Wisconsin 89
Syracuse, New York 37

Team USA 65
Texas City, Texas 103
Texas-Louisiana League 111, 113, 143, 145
Thom, Bruce 116
Thompson, James "Shag" 62–64
Three-I League 63, 101
Thunder Bay, Ontario 86, 87, 89, 90, 91, 97, 98, 100, 109
Thunder Bay Whiskey Jacks 4, 90, 104, 107, 108, 120, 141, 167
Toronto Metros 26
Toronto, Ontario, Blue Jays 26, 27, 29, 148
Tremblay, Jean 139
Trinity College 63
Trois-Rivières, Quebec 137, 148, 149
Twin Ports League 89

University at Albany 144
University of North Carolina 49, 62, 63, 78, 82
University of Virginia 6, 22
Union Paper Company 14
United League 145
USA Today 129
Utica, New York Blue Sox 57, 59, 103

Vance, Marilyn 52, 54
Vancouver, British Columbia 42, 43
Van Schaack, Tom 105
Veeck, Bill 99
Veeck, Mike 95, 98, 99, 100, 105, 106, 120
Veeck as in Wreck 99
Verdi, Frank 104
Victoria, British Columbia 25, 43, 103
Vietnam War 6, 7

Wade Stadium 88, 89, 96, 97
Wake Forest University 34
Ward, Jay 135, 136
Washington Senators 16, 93
Weaver, Claude "Buck" 56
West Palm Beach, Florida 44
Western Carolinas League 27, 28, 29, 32
Western League 63, 113, 120
Westrum, Wes 40
White Rock, British Columbia 124, 126
Wild and Outside 106
Wildgoose, Lyle 82, 85
Willson, Meredith 1
Winn, Kevin 143
Winnipeg, Manitoba 92, 93, 115, 117, 134, 138, 145
Winnipeg Goldeyes 4, 122, 141, 145, 155
Wolf, Wally 16
Wolff, Claire 61, 81, 135, 163
Wolff, Hoffman 61, 81, 108, 135, 144, 163
Wolff, Michelle Guimond 61, 68, 69, 81, 121, 131, 157, 158, 159, 163
Wolfson Stadium 32, 33
Worcester, Massachusetts 147
World Football League 32

Young, Andy 84, 85

Zebulon, North Carolina 71

www.ingramcontent.com/pod-product-compliance
Ingram Content Group UK Ltd.
Pitfield, Milton Keynes, MK11 3LW, UK
UKHW042015140426
5217IPUK00015B/1187